KU-304-202

Contents

Introduction

If you are reading this book, you are probably one of the thousands who join the community of family carers every year, and you might be looking for the answer to one question: 'What will life be like from now on?'

You may have been warned that caring for someone elderly, ill or disabled can be very difficult. True. But this is only half of the truth. Being a carer is also, and most importantly, one of the most rewarding jobs there is. Why? Because it gives you the chance to make a real difference in the life of the person in your care, and because it will enrich you emotionally while you give them hope, comfort and joy.

This book gives you practical, step-by-step advice on how you can achieve all of this. It aims to tell you how to help the person in your care in a manner that fosters their independence, dignity and self respect, as well as protecting you from stress and burnout. The information is drawn from the latest research in the field of caring, which has been stripped of the jargon to make it easy to read and understand by anyone.

In this book, you will find:

- Information about skills for being a good carer, the challenges and rewards of caring and pitfalls to avoid.

- Strategies for dealing with the diagnosis.

- Details about benefits and other financial help, as well as practical and emotional support available to carers.

- Advice for young carers, including a list of contacts for children and teenagers looking after a relative who may want to talk with someone about their situation.

- How to take care of yourself, including lifestyle advice and examples of relaxation exercises.

- Caring strategies for different groups – people with a physical disability, vision or hearing loss, mental illness, the elderly and those at the end of life. These groups are dealt with in separate chapters.

At the end of the book, there is a help list section followed by the references section. These include the details of organisations as well as articles and books mentioned in the various chapters if you wish to find out more on any particular topic mentioned.

Disclaimer

This book is for general information only. It is not intended to replace professional medical advice. Although every care has been taken to ensure accuracy, you should always consult a healthcare professional before using any of the information contained in this book, because of constantly changing guidelines, medical recommendations and research findings.

Chapter One
Being a Carer

If you are new to caring, you may like to know that you are not alone. You have just joined a community of over five million people, which increases by about 6,000 individuals every day. The overall number of carers in the UK is expected to rise to a staggering nine million by 2037.

Extraordinary people

The caring community is no ordinary community. It is made up of individuals with extraordinary skills, energy and generosity, who take care of other human beings as a mere act of love and compassion. It includes people of any age, many of whom have health problems themselves, as well as family and work responsibilities.

To get a real sense of the remarkable qualities of family carers across the country, you just need to take a look at the following facts.

According to the Office of National Statistics:

- Of family carers, 1 in 5 provides care to an ill or disabled relative, friend or partner for more than 50 hours a week. Consider that, on average, people in paid positions in the UK work no more than 37.5 hours per week.

- Of those providing care for more than 50 hours per week, half are over the age of 55 and experiencing some health problems themselves.

- About 1.6 million full-time employees are also family carers.

- Approximately 250,000 disabled or chronically ill people are family carers.

(Source: Office of National Statistics, 2003.)

'The caring community is no ordinary community. It is made up of individuals with extraordinary skills, energy and generosity.'

So what are you going to do?

As you begin your journey as a carer, you are probably wondering, 'Where do I start? How do I take care of my loved one?'

Being able to understand and share your loved one's feelings is one of the most important qualities you can have. Many ill or disabled people often isolate themselves, which is why empathy is so crucial – it helps you to stay emotionally in contact with your loved one and, in turn, prevent their isolation.

Put yourself in their shoes

For some carers, empathy is an innate quality. It just comes naturally to them. Others need to learn what being an empathetic carer means and how to be one. If you belong to this group, here is an easy way to understand the true meaning and value of empathy: try to imagine what and how you would feel if you were in the place of your loved one.

Among other things, it is likely you would feel sad for the way your illness affects your life. You may also feel frustrated as you become aware that you will no longer be able to do things you like. The simple act of placing yourself in the shoes of a disabled or ill person will help you understand what your loved one is going through, and the enormous challenges they face. You will be better able to understand their feelings.

Respect their preferences

This concept is at the very heart of what is known among experts as 'person-centred' care; that is, care based around the specific needs and preferences of a person.

We all have our special ways of doing things – small habits that we are likely to keep for life – and we don't want to abandon them. Together with our character and personal history they make us what we are. They make us unique. A person with an illness or disability is no different – you always need to keep this in mind when caring for your loved one. Know what they like and don't like, and do everything possible to respect their wishes.

Avoid changes if the person is comfortable with a certain routine; this will save them the frustration of having to cope with new, unfamiliar situations. For example, if your loved one used to take showers, don't change to baths only because you think bathing is easier. Rather, find ways that make it possible for them to continue taking showers. Maybe you could use a chair so they can sit while being washed to make the experience easy, safe and possible. Don't stop offering your loved one their favourite dish because they no longer have the fine motor skills (the ability to co-ordinate small muscle movements, e.g. the use of fingers) required to use a knife and fork. Cut the food into small bite-sized pieces and allow them to eat with their fingers instead. These are examples of the practical actions needed to give your loved one person-centred care.

Case study

'Dad used to start the day reading the newspaper while having coffee. But his vision was getting worse and worse. He was feeling frustrated because he couldn't read well anymore, so I started having breakfast with him. Every morning, we have coffee and a little chat, and then I read the newspaper to him. Half an hour – that's all it takes. And he is in a much better mood for the rest of the day.'

Antonia, aged 52.

Give them choice

Of course, you need to know the person's preferences in order to provide them with person-centred care. If you are a close relative, son, daughter or partner, you probably know them well. If you are not, you need to ask the person, or their family and friends, how they would like things to be done for them.

Even if the person has dementia, ask them directly. Professor Dawn Brooker of Worcester University says: 'Although people may lose the capacity to make truly informed choices about abstract decisions [like deciding whether to visit a friend or call them on the phone], the evidence is that people can make reliable decisions about long-held preferences well into their dementia.'

So, remember to ask your loved one about anything that can make their life easier and more enjoyable. Give them as many choices and options as possible. Make sure you know:

- What they would like to eat, drink and wear.
- Their preferred time for having breakfast, watching TV, listening to the radio and so on.
- What they would like to do during the day.
- Where they would like to have their daily walk.
- Whom they would like to visit and spend time with.

It's also crucial to have them make decisions about anything that matters to them. This will give them a sense of control over their life, and enable them to feel important.

'Good carers also treat the persons in their care with the same respect and dignity they would expect for themselves.'

Ensure dignity and respect

Good carers also treat the persons in their care with the same respect and dignity they would expect for themselves. They:

- Respect the person's need for privacy, especially when providing personal care.
- Talk with them as one adult to another.
- Keep them informed about anything that concerns them.
- Always say please and thank you.

The importance of cherished possessions

Some people requiring full-time assistance move in with their carers. When this happens, space constraints often limit the number of personal objects the person being cared for can bring with them. Yet experts say it is important that carers make sure their loved ones continue to be surrounded by their favourite personal possessions, like photographs, letters, books, cards and so on. Work by researchers at the University of Tromsø in Norway and the University of Auckland in New Zealand shows that since such possessions are often reminders of important relationships, favourite familiar events and past achievements, they are important to help individuals maintain their sense of identity and emotional wellbeing. This is especially at times of major upheaval, for example moving house (Kroger and Adair, 2008).

Make them feel loved

Whatever the illness or disability of the person in your care, you need to be able to communicate your affection and dedication at all times. A hug, a cuddle or a gentle stroke on their hands can work wonders to ensure they feel loved, safe and important.

Don't let a day go by without saying 'I love you'.

Challenges...

Caring for a loved one can be emotionally and physically challenging. This is particularly the case if you have other day-to-day commitments and responsibilities. You may have to juggle many things every day. Depending on your personal circumstances, you will have to make a real effort to combine your caring tasks with going to work, doing housework, looking after children, shopping, attending doctors' appointments and so on, sometimes without a break. There will be times when you will feel like giving up.

The challenge is even greater if you did not plan to be a carer, but have unexpectedly become one because someone in your family had an accident, suffered a stroke, had a fall, or was diagnosed with a terminal illness. It will take time to adjust to the new situation, and you will need to be strong enough to be able to help your loved one do the same.

...And rewards

So, is it all bad news? Undoubtedly, being a carer is one of the most difficult and demanding jobs. But ask any experienced carer and they will tell you, without hesitation, that the rewards always outweigh the challenges.

In fact, caring for an ill or disabled loved one will enrich your life in many, and unexpected, ways. Most carers say that attending to the needs of the person in their care has become an important part of their life, because it makes them feel useful. It gives purpose to their life.

Most carers gain a great sense of satisfaction and reward in knowing that, thanks to their continuous dedication, their loved one can continue to live with their family, rather going to a hospital or care home. For many, being a carer is also a precious opportunity to renew a relationship that has gone through difficult times. Others have found that caring has given them more chances to develop new friendships through support groups and other resources. As a result, they are now enjoying, with their loved one, a richer and more stimulating social life.

'All too often, carers push themselves to the edge. This is, without exception, the most common mistake made by the millions of people caring for an elderly, ill or disabled loved one, and should be avoided.'

Common pitfalls to avoid

All too often, carers push themselves to the edge. This is, without exception, the most common mistake made by the millions of people caring for an elderly, ill or disabled loved one, and should be avoided. If you are becoming a carer, you may feel like you should put all your time and energy into caring.

The problem is that if you don't get enough sleep, and don't take time to relax and have fun, you put yourself at risk of serious health problems, both physical and mental. This will make it impossible for you to continue to look after your loved one.

You may need to be a carer for many years – maybe more than a decade if, for example, the person in your care has Alzheimer's disease. If you want to fulfil your role, you must start by taking good care of yourself, right from the beginning. The next chapter will tell you in detail how you can do this, without decreasing the quality of the care you provide.

Drifting into isolation is another frequent mistake. Some carers simply lock themselves and their loved one apart from the rest of the world, refusing any opportunity to go out. Fear of stigma is one reason, especially among carers of people with dementia. However, more generally, carers begin avoiding friends and relatives because they wrongly assume that their loved one's condition does not allow for a normal social life. And yet, interacting with others is vital in a caring situation. It helps to prevent both the carer and the person being cared for from slipping into loneliness and depression.

With this in mind, try not to anticipate the worst. For instance, avoid declining an invitation to eat out because you think your loved one will not cope with it. Rather, find information on how to make the experience comfortable, pleasant and safe, and just try it! You'll give your loved one an all-important opportunity for enjoying other people's company, and it will take your mind off your worries for a while.

Find support

One way to reduce your risk of isolation is to join support groups and relevant organisations, such as Carers UK (see help list). You will have the opportunity to meet other carers with whom to share feelings, views and experiences. Having an extended social network will also make things easier to cope with, especially at particularly difficult times.

There is still place for joy

The fact is, no matter how difficult your circumstances are, there will still be moments to treasure. There will still be smiles and tender memories to cherish. Mostly, this will depend on your attitude; it will be easier if you tend to see the positive side of things and do your best to lighten up the atmosphere when needed. The benefits will go both ways. A recent study, led by Tracy Tan of Wilfrid Laurier University in Canada, found that a positive attitude and using humour sensitively can increase levels of happiness among people with Alzheimer's disease and reduce their carers' risk of stress and burnout.

'The fact is, no matter how difficult your circumstances are, there will still be moments to treasure.'

Summing Up

As you become a family carer, you may want to consider the key qualities that will ensure you take the best possible care of your loved one:

- Be an empathetic carer – show you understand and share their feelings.

- Provide care that meets their preferences – know what they like and make them happy.

- Give your loved one control over their life – offer them choices and let them make their own decisions.

- Ensure dignity – respect their privacy and keep them informed about things that matter to them.

- Understand the importance of personal possessions – let them keep cherished objects.

- Make them feel important – show your love with small acts of affection, and say 'I love you'.

- Don't push yourself to the limit – set aside time for rest and leisure.

- Avoid isolation – keep yourself and your loved one involved in social activities. Join support groups and organisations.

- Try to see things from a positive perspective and use humour to lighten up the mood – a happy attitude will be beneficial to both of you.

- Keep in mind that although carers face great challenges, the rewards are greater. There is nothing more rewarding than being able to put a smile on the face of an unwell loved one.

Chapter Two
Life After Diagnosis

Some family carers take up the responsibility of looking after someone who was already ill, and whose health has so deteriorated that they can no longer take care of themselves.

Many others become carers after a close relative has been diagnosed with a disabling disease, or suffered a serious accident. In this case, there is an additional emotional burden to consider. Usually, the person being cared for goes into shock. Their life is suddenly being turned upside down, and they are overwhelmed by disbelief, confusion and fear.

They need you

As a close relative or friend, you are probably feeling exactly the same. But as a carer, you have to pull yourself together fairly quickly and carry on – no matter what. You need to give your loved one the strength to start their new journey, and to do so with hope and resilience. This is often easier if you encourage them to talk about their feelings and you show you understand what they are going through. Spend quality time with them, and keep your promises. If you say you will take a walk together later in the day, do it.

A whole new life

You may need to plan ahead and organise a whole new life for the person in your care and for yourself. You may need to deal with the practicalities, such as finding specialists, obtaining medical information and dealing with financial matters. In addition, you will need to rearrange your work, family and social life around your caring responsibilities. All this while providing your loved one with the practical and emotional help they need.

'You need to give your loved one the strength to start their new journey, and to do so with hope and resilience.'

Fighting back

Adapting to a diagnosis, new life and a new routine is a particularly delicate time. The initial sense of disbelief usually turns into sadness, and your loved one may gradually withdraw from activities and friends. You, as their carer, can make the difference between them spiralling into depression or rising up to the challenge and fighting back. The key is to help them find new meaning and a sense of purpose in their life. The two case studies below show how this can happen.

Case study

'After the diagnosis, my wife gave up most of the things she used to do – no more trips to the shops, walks, visits to the church, bridge nights.

'As a husband, you can either sit there and watch, or do something to help. My wife was a nurse, so I spoke with the people at the hospital where she used to work.

'Now she does some volunteering work there, helping others with her illness, but more severely affected. She loves it. She says helping others is wonderful, because it makes her feel like she is doing something for herself, instead of giving up and hiding away.'

Michael, aged 68.

Case study

'When Peter heard he had Parkinson's, he just took it like a death sentence. He didn't even want to take his medicines. He couldn't see the point.

'I felt so frustrated that one day I just snapped. "So what are we going to do?" I said. "Are we going to just cry and feel sad for the rest of our life, or are we going to do something about it, and make the most of what we have got?"

'I felt very bad for what I had just said. But, somehow, those words hit him. Since then, he's started spending more and more time with our family, especially our grandchildren. Of course, he continues to have his highs and lows, but he really tries to make the most of every single day.'

Ann, aged 61.

Planning ahead

As reality begins to sink in, you need to consider encouraging your loved one to make arrangements for the future. This is particularly important if they have been diagnosed with dementia. Early in the course of the illness, the sufferer retains their cognitive faculties (i.e. sense, imagination, memory and understanding) and can still make their own decisions. But this will not be possible once their condition starts deteriorating.

Here are some of the things they may want to consider:

- Writing down preferences about the type of care they want to receive, should they lose the capacity to make decisions. This is called an 'Advanced Statement'. It is not legally binding but can give peace of mind.

- Deciding what medical treatments they don't want to receive in the future. This is called an 'Advanced Decision' and is legally binding.

- Claiming benefits to which they and/or you are entitled (see also chapter 3).

- Making a will. This can still be changed if your loved one wishes to do so.

- Putting their legal and financial affairs in order.

'As reality begins to sink in, you need to consider encouraging your loved one to make arrangements for the future.'

■ Setting up direct debits to ensure that bills are regularly paid.

You and your loved one's GP

From now on, your loved one will need to see their GP regularly for physical examinations and tests. This is important to ensure they are responding to treatments and to identify early signs of complications or side effects from medication. The GP will give you invaluable help and advice to make important decisions and deal with problems as the disease progresses. They are also the best first source of information about the illness or disability of the person in your care.

Below is a list of questions your loved one may want to ask their GP after the diagnosis.

■ What do my test results actually show?

■ How serious is my condition?

■ Which medications can help with it?

■ Are there any non-pharmacological or alternative treatments I should try?

■ What can I do to lessen the symptoms?

■ Where can I find out more about my condition?

■ Do you have any leaflets or pamphlets about it?

■ Are there any organisations I can contact for help and support?

■ What should I expect as the disease progresses?

■ What skills or abilities will I lose first, and which ones will I retain?

Remember, in order for the GP to be able to develop a care plan that best suits your loved one's specific situation and needs, it is important that he or she knows the following:

■ Medications, supplements or herbal remedies your loved one is taking.

■ Changes in health, body weight or behaviour that you or your loved one may have noticed.

'Avoid missing GP appointments, and follow their instructions carefully. You may want to take a notebook with you and write notes before leaving the surgery.'

- Anything that may concern you or your loved one.

Avoid missing GP appointments, and follow their instructions carefully. You may want to take a notebook with you and write notes before leaving the surgery.

Breaking the news

Patients may receive their diagnosis from a doctor or a close relative. In both cases, it is important to break the news in the most appropriate way to avoid negative reactions.

According to a study of 151 carers, patients and nurses, published in the journal *Cancer Nursing* (Rassin, 2006), patients should:

- Be informed as soon as possible and not be lied to.

- Be encouraged to express their emotions.

- Be able to decide on the amount of information they receive, especially with respect to sensitive issues such as how long they are expected to live.

In breaking the news, doctors and carers should:

- Provide comfort and reassurance through caring gestures, such as hugging or holding hands.

- Avoid negative statements like: 'There is nothing more we can do' or 'I am afraid I have bad news'.

- Use positive statements. Michal Rassin, the study's lead researcher says: 'The sentences that greatly helped patients to cope with the situation… were the following: "I'll be there for you" and "I admire your courage".'

At some point, family and friends will also need to be informed. It is important that this is done only when your loved one is comfortable with the idea. They may want to break the news themselves, or ask you to do so. In both cases, consider that you don't have to give more information than you want.

'At some point, family and friends will also need to be informed. It is important that this is done only when your loved one is comfortable with the idea.'

Summing Up

After the diagnosis, your loved one may feel like their life will never be the same again. You can help them find reasons for fighting back and looking at the future with optimism. Here are some pointers:

- Encourage your loved one to talk about how they feel and share their emotions.
- Help them claim any benefits they are entitled to and put legal and financial matters in order. They may also want to make a will and write down their wishes regarding treatments they would like to receive – or refuse – in the future.
- Make the most of appointments with the GP.
- Ensure news of the diagnosis is given in the most appropriate way.

Chapter Three

Help is at Hand

Carers face all sorts of challenges – financial, practical and emotional – for which they need support. This chapter gives an overview of what help is available and where to find it.

Benefits

If you are new to caring, you may not know which benefits you and your loved one are entitled to. Your local Citizens Advice Bureau, Carers UK and the government website Directgov are good sources of information (see help list).

Benefits for carers include (but are not limited to):

- Carer's Allowance – a weekly payment for carers who look after someone for at least 35 hours a week.

- Direct payments for carers – money the local council awards if you are assessed as needing support with caring for your loved one.

- Help with pensions, if you cannot afford to contribute enough towards your pension.

Benefits for the carers or person being cared for include (but are not limited to):

- Housing Benefit – helps you, or the person in your care, pay for the rent if you are on low income.

- Council Tax Benefit – if you, or the person in your care, need help to pay council tax.

- There is also a Disability Living Allowance available for those who have a disability and need a carer.

'If you are new to caring, you may not know which benefits you and your loved one are entitled to. Your local Citizens Advice Bureau, Carers UK and the government website Directgov are good sources of information.'

A guide to financial help for carers including the full list of benefits available can be found at www.direct.gov.uk. Consider that, once obtained, certain benefits allow you to receive further help, such as discounts on taxes and medicines. So, even though the claiming process may require some time, it is worth applying.

Other financial support

You and the person in your care may also be entitled to receive financial help for transport. This can be in the form of:

- Discount railcards.

- Bus passes.

- Parking benefits for disabled people and their carers through the Blue Badge parking scheme.

- Help to buy a car through the Motability car scheme.

In addition, your loved one may be entitled to receive benefits to help them with fuel bills during the winter months. If they are blind or have severe sight loss, they only pay half of the amount due for a TV licence. There are also schemes to help disabled people buy a wheelchair.

Practical help

Financial support, of course, can make things easier, but you will also need practical help – people ready to listen if you need a sympathetic ear, and to take your place when you feel you need a break from it for a while.

Family and work

Most carers find help among relatives, friends and colleagues. Don't wait for them to come forward – they may feel like they are intruding, or fear that by offering help they are implying that you can't cope with your caring responsibilities. Some may not even know that you have become a full-time carer. So, don't hesitate to ask.

There are many ways in which friends, relatives and colleagues can help. They may want to take your loved one out for a walk, do errands for you, drive your children to places or make a meal for you. Whatever they choose to do, their support is crucial. It allows you to have your own life while looking after your loved one, and this, as discussed in chapter 5, is paramount to avoiding stress and being a good carer.

Social services

As you become a carer, you should inform your local social services. They will look into ways of giving you practical help. For example, they can provide someone to help you at home with certain caring tasks, like assisting your loved one with eating or bathing.

They can also arrange things so that you can have a break from caring for a while. This can happen in a number of ways. Your loved one may be offered the chance to attend a local day centre, which may include social activities, clubs and trips, or you may receive help to pay for respite care. This means that the person in your care will stay for a short period of time in a care home, so you can have a holiday to recharge yourself.

Social services are part of your local council. If you don't know how to contact them, ask your GP.

Emotional support

Several studies suggest that when it comes to ways of helping carers cope with their everyday challenges, emotional support is essential. In fact, a study by a team of researchers led by Bart Osse, of the University of Nijmegen in The Netherlands, found that the need for addressing emotional burden is a top priority for carers. The vast majority rely on family and friends to share feelings, fears and concerns to alleviate their emotional burden. Support groups also have an important role; these groups offer carers invaluable opportunities to meet other carers who can fully understand the challenges they are going through.

'As you become a carer, you should inform your local social services. They will look into ways of giving you practical help.'

Summing Up

- Several benefits are available to carers and the person in their care to help them pay for, among other things, rent, taxes, home help, fuel bills and transportation.

- Practical help is also available. Relatives, friends and even colleagues will be happy to help if you ask them.

- Social services offer respite and day care programmes that allow carers to take breaks from caring.

- Support groups can help alleviate the emotional burden of caring.

Chapter Four

Young Carers

A young carer is a child or teenager who provides emotional or physical help, or both, to a family member with an illness, disability or addiction to alcohol or drugs.

As a young carer, you may have to do things that people of your age don't normally do. For this reason, you may struggle to keep up with your school commitments. You may also find it difficult to spend time with friends and participate in fun activities. This chapter tells you how to lead as normal a life as possible, how to deal with the most common problems and where to get help when you need it.

Share your feelings and take care

As with adult carers, once you become a carer your health may be at risk as a result of stress, worries and anxiety. Sharing your feelings with your best friend, a family member or relative, one of your teachers or a counsellor can help you stay healthy.

Additional ways in which carers can protect themselves against the consequences of stress are described in chapter 5. In short, it all comes down to one simple thing: always remember to take good care of yourself. Find the time to do things you like, keep physically active, enjoy the company of your friends and eat healthily.

'As a young carer, you may have to do things that people of your age don't normally do.'

The importance of friends and fun

Being a carer at a young age may mean missing out on some of the activities and fun that children and teenagers enjoy. This can result in isolation, feelings of loneliness and may, ultimately, lead to depression. Therefore, keeping your friends and developing new ones so you can continue to share with them some fun time is of paramount importance.

A good source of help is the Young Carers Project (YCP). The YCP is an initiative of the Princess Royal Trust for Carers offering children and teenagers with caring responsibilities the opportunity to participate in social activities, sports events, summer holidays, weekends away, shopping trips and more. The YCP gives you the chance to meet other young carers with whom you can share feelings, worries and everyday experiences. You can also talk with someone older for help and advice on how to deal with a particular problem. To find out more, visit the YCP's website (see help list).

'The Princess Royal Trust for Carers has also developed a charter of rights for children and teenagers who are family carers.'

You have rights

The Princess Royal Trust for Carers has also developed a charter of rights for children and teenagers who are family carers. Getting help from schools or employers so you can continue your education or keep your job while looking after a relative is one of the rights you are entitled to.

Other rights set out by the charter include:

▪ The right to be listened to.

▪ The right to have free time from caring.

▪ The right to receive practical help.

▪ The right to make decisions on things that matter to you.

▪ The right to have access to useful information.

▪ The right to have someone who supports your cause.

▪ The right to know how to make a complaint.

It's your choice

Remember that you don't have to be a carer if you don't want to: it's your legal right. You also have the right to choose the amount of time you want to dedicate to caring. The person in your care may be eligible to receive help from social services, once their conditions and circumstances have been assessed, so they don't have to rely completely on you.

Don't feel like you are letting down your loved one; if you don't want to become their carer, it may be the best thing for them as you may not be able to provide the same level and quality of care as an adult or regular carer. If you have doubts about becoming a carer, or feel under pressure to become one, you can contact Childline to talk about your thoughts and feelings (see help list).

Tip

If you find it difficult to speak to an adult about your situation at home, write down what you want to say in a letter.

Coping with school life

Being a carer may affect your school performance because you may not be able to attend every day, or have enough time to complete your homework. The best way to deal with this is to talk with your teachers. Be open and specific with them. Explain what your family situation is and which problems you have in particular. They will be able to help you in many ways.

- They may be able to provide out-of-school-hours teaching if you are missing lessons.

- They may take steps to ensure you can participate more regularly in school activities.

- They may allow you to call home from school to make sure that the person in your care is okay.

- They may look into acts of bullying you may be experiencing.

'Remember that you don't have to be a carer if you don't want to: it's your legal right. You also have the right to choose the amount of time you want to dedicate to caring.'

This will relieve a lot of the pressure you are under. As a result, you may be less anxious and worried, and have more chance of doing well at school. You will be a better carer too.

Getting help with job commitments

A job may help you cope better financially with your situation and allow you to build your future. However, due to caring responsibilities, you may find it difficult to perform well; you may need to take days off regularly, arrive late, miss meetings and so on. If you don't tell your boss that you are a carer, they may not understand your behaviour and you may lose your job. For this reason, it is important that you let them know about your situation as soon as possible. They should be happy to help you in any way they can – they may allow you to work flexible hours, for example. They may reduce your workload, or assign you a helper. As a result, you will be better able to combine your work with your caring responsibilities without the need to give up your job.

Who can help?

As a young person, you may sometimes find yourself dealing with a problem that is too difficult to handle. Remember, help is never too far away. Talk with your GP, school nurse or social services. They can, and want, to help you.

There are also several organisations that provide practical support and advice to young carers. These can:

- Give you information about the health problem of the person in your care, and how to deal with it.

- Help you find friends and participate in fun activities.

- Give you tips on how to make your life easier, at home and at school.

So, if you have a question, are in difficulty or simply want to talk to someone who understands your situation, contact one of the following:

- YCP.

- Carers Direct.

- Childline.

- Samaritans.

Contact details for these organisations can be found in the help list.

Case study

'My aunt developed dementia when I was 16 years old. My mum and dad were working at that time, so my grandmother and I took care of her. At school, I was finding it difficult to keep up with the rest of the class. Then I told my maths teacher and things changed completely – for the better! She arranged for five of my friends to take turns coming to my house after school. They would look after my aunt for an hour, so that I could concentrate on my homework. If I missed a lesson, they would call or visit to tell me what they had done so I could catch up in the evening.'

Betty, aged 29.

Summing Up

Caring for an ill or disabled person at a young age can make it hard to lead a normal life. Without the right support, your school and social life and, therefore, your future may be at risk. So, tell the adults you trust that you are a carer. They should give you the help you need.

Also:

■ Talk with someone about your situation and how you feel about it. You will find that this can relieve some of the pressure you may be under. Looking after yourself is crucial.

■ Understand the importance of keeping your friends and making new ones.

■ Contact organisations like the YCP for social and sport activities available to young carers in your area.

■ As with adults, young carers have rights. Among other things, these include the right to receive practical help, make decisions and complaints, and be provided with relevant information.

■ Remember that you have the right to choose not to become a carer, if you don't want to.

■ Talk to your teacher if you are finding it difficult to cope with your school commitments. If you have a job, tell your boss that you are also a family carer.

■ Whenever you feel that the pressure is too much, ask for help. Your GP, school nurse, social services and other organisations are there to help you.

Chapter Five

Caring for the Carer

There is one thing carers often tend to forget: that taking care of themselves is as important as taking care of their loved one. Carers carry out an extremely demanding job, so you need to refresh your mind and body to avoid stress and fatigue in order to continue to provide your loved one with the care they need. Yet, most carers fail to recognise this, or do it too late when symptoms of stress and burnout are already showing.

Although the terms stress and burnout are often used interchangeably, they are not the same thing. Stress is the pressure we experience when confronted with events we feel unable to deal with, whereas burnout is a medical condition that develops as a result of being exposed to stress for some time. The consequences of prolonged exposure to stress can be quite serious.

Brigid Duffy, a clinical psychologist at Wolverhampton Primary Care Trust, says: 'Family caregivers are faced with persistent demands over an extended period of time, and have been found to experience a high level of burden associated with high expressed emotion, depression, anxiety and difficulties in coping.'

Recognising burnout

According to recent studies, both stress and burnout can lead to serious health problems, including cancer, heart attack, stroke, depression, diabetes and hypertension. And carers should do everything possible to avoid them.

Below are the most common signs and symptoms of burnout. Take a careful look at the list and check anything that applies to you. If you are experiencing any of the following problems, you should see your GP:

- Feelings of helplessness, frustration or anger.
- Difficulty concentrating and remembering things.

'Stress is the pressure we experience when confronted with events we feel unable to deal with, whereas burnout is a medical condition that develops as a result of being exposed to stress for some time.'

- Anxiety, especially at night.
- Irritability.
- A tendency to withdraw from social and family life.
- Loss of interest in activities you used to enjoy.
- Eating too much or too little.
- Excessive alcohol or caffeine consumption.
- Smoking too much.

In addition, you may experience difficulty sleeping and chronic fatigue. Your immune system may weaken and you may start feeling ill more often than normal.

Tip

Learn about your loved one's condition or disability. You may want to read books, watch videos and TV programmes, attend events and take classes. This will help reduce your risk of burnout by improving your confidence in your ability to provide the right care.

A recent study found that of 61 carers of people with dementia, those who knew the least about the condition felt insecure about their caring abilities, and this put them at increased risk of stress and burnout (Duffy et al., 2009).

Take good care of yourself

Prevention is, of course, the best approach. The following strategies can help you keep stress at bay and reduce your risk of burnout.

- Dedicate time to yourself – set aside a few minutes a day for doing things you enjoy and that help you relax. Examples include listening to music, reading or taking a bubble bath.

- Take up a hobby – gardening, cooking, dancing, playing an instrument and painting are just a few ideas. But with a little imagination and creativity, the possibilities are endless.

- Spend time with family and friends – for example, eat out or go to the cinema. Do something you enjoy at least once a week.

- Ask other family members for help – they may want to look after your loved one at least once in a while, thus reducing your burden.

- Find a respite centre near you – this will give your loved one the opportunity to meet and socialise with others, and you will have some free time to relax.

- Tell your GP that you are a carer – they will ensure you receive regular health checks. They will also be able to refer you to other services, like counselling and support groups. See chapter 3 for more information on practical help available to carers from social services.

- For support and advice on ways that you can get short breaks from caring, contact Carers UK or The Princess Royal Trust for Carers (see help list).

Use relaxation

Another good way to prevent stress and burnout is to use relaxation techniques. There are several you can easily integrate into your daily routine. Below are three of the most common.

'For maximum effect, do your relaxation exercises in a quiet place, where there are no distractions.'

Tip

For maximum effect, do your relaxation exercises in a quiet place, where there are no distractions.

Deep breathing exercises

- Breathe in slowly and deeply through the nose.

- Hold your breath for a few moments.

- Slowly breathe out through the mouth.
- Repeat a few times.

An advantage of deep breathing exercises is that they can easily be performed anywhere, at any time, either sitting or standing – or laying on your back before going to sleep.

Progressive muscle relaxation

- Sit in a dining chair with your feet flat on the floor.
- Stretch your legs. Then focus on each muscle, starting from the toes. Contract the muscle, hold for a few seconds and relax.
- Do the same with the muscles of your arms – tighten and relax each muscle, starting from your fingers.
- Repeat for face, chest and back.

Benson relaxation technique

- Sit in a comfortable chair with your eyes closed.
- While breathing normally, relax all of your body, from your face down to your toes.
- Think of a number every time you breathe out.
- Continue for up to 15 or 20 minutes.

Think positive

According to research, another way to protect yourself from stress is to think positively no matter what the circumstances are. This may sound like it's easier said than done, but the following points may be helpful in trying it.

- Change your attitude towards situations and events that you perceive as too difficult to deal with. Try to see them in the right perspective. For example, if at the end of the day you feel overwhelmed and believe you can't cope anymore, imagine that, no matter how hard your day has been, tomorrow will not be as difficult as today.

- Don't blame yourself if your loved one has had a bad day or couldn't eat or sleep well. Accept the idea that, despite your efforts, sometimes certain strategies simply don't work, and this is for a variety of reasons that may have nothing to do with you.

- Learn to see things in shades of grey, rather than in black or white. Nothing and no one is absolutely perfect. If you start thinking this way, you will be able to remain optimistic and you will find value in everything you do, rather than feeling constantly disappointed if you think about how you could have done things better.

Stay healthy

Lastly, keep healthy. It will help you better cope with stressful situations and prevent them from getting out of control. There are three things, in particular, that you should do:

- Choose the right food.

- Keep active.

- Eliminate bad habits, such as smoking, drinking too much alcohol or sleeping too little.

'Learn to see things in shades of grey, rather than in black or white. Nothing and no one is absolutely perfect.'

Tip

A recent study published in the journal *Environmental Science and Technology* shows that exercise is more effective at preventing stress when performed in a green space, like a park or garden (Barton and Pretty, 2010).

The list overleaf gives you an idea of what helps to maintain a healthy body. Take a look at your lifestyle and compare it with the recommendations given. Then, focus on the things you need to change.

- Exercise regularly – this doesn't necessarily mean enrolling in a strenuous exercise programme, a 20-minute walk on most weekdays can do wonders.

- Ensure your diet is varied and well balanced – your meals should mostly consist of fresh fruit and vegetables, plus smaller amounts of grains, fish, meat (preferably white) and dairy foods. This will ensure that your body receives, every day, all the nutrients (e.g. sugars, proteins, vitamins and minerals) that it needs to function at its best.

- Eat moderately – try having several light snacks during the day, instead of two heavy meals.

Also, try to sleep for at least eight hours per night. If you have difficulties, try the following:

- Go to bed every night at the same time.

- Don't use your bedroom for working.

- Avoid reading anything heavy-going or watching the TV while in bed.

- Don't drink, eat or exercise too much just before bedtime.

- If you don't fall asleep within 15 to 20 minutes, get up from bed and go into another room. Go back only when you feel sleepy.

- Eliminate daytime naps. If you cannot avoid them, sleep for less than half an hour, and always before 3pm.

For more information on sleep problems see *Insomnia – The Essential Guide* (Need2Know).

Summing Up

Your wellbeing is just as precious as the wellbeing of the person in your care. Just stop and think for a moment – if you become ill, who will take care of your loved one? Who will do things for them in that very special way that only you can do?

Besides, as we have seen in this chapter, taking good care of yourself is nothing complicated. Just follow these simple steps:

- Use relaxation techniques.
- Adopt a healthy lifestyle – exercise regularly, eat the right food in the right amounts and try to get enough sleep.
- Find support from voluntary groups and health services.
- Ask for help from family, friends and your GP.
- Dedicate at least a few minutes a day to things you enjoy doing.

'Your wellbeing is just as precious as the wellbeing of the person in your care.'

Chapter Six

Caring for the Physically Disabled

According to the Disabled Living Foundation (DLF), there are more than 10 million people with a physical disability in the UK. Of these, half are older adults over the age of 65 and approximately 800,000 are children. This chapter describes simple strategies that carers can use to help someone with a disability remain active and independent, and avoid most common complications such as pressure ulcers and depression.

Exercise

Don't assume that since your loved one has lost their mobility, they cannot exercise – they can, and should. Regular exercise is key to mental and physical wellbeing. It makes our body stronger, improves our immune system and protects us from life-threatening diseases. Research has repeatedly shown that this is true at any age and for any medical condition. Therefore, there is no reason why people with a disability should not take advantage of the many benefits of exercise.

Gentle exercise of the upper body is possible in most cases. For example, dancing can be done if the person is encouraged to move their arms and hands to the rhythm of the music. If your loved one is looking for more thrill and excitement, there is a wide range of outdoor sports they can try, including horse riding, cycling, fishing and so on. And, of course, team sports like basketball, volleyball and more.

'Regular exercise is key to mental and physical wellbeing. It makes our body stronger, improves our immune system and protects us from life-threatening diseases.'

The best way to start is to visit your GP. He or she will assess your loved one's conditions to make sure they are fit to exercise. They will refer you to a physical therapist, who will develop an exercise plan tailored to your loved one and based on their abilities.

Tip

When caring for people with a physical impairment, or any other condition that limits their ability to perform everyday activities, provide help in a way that respects their need for independence. Step in only when necessary or if explicitly asked to do so.

Grooming – wheelchair users

For wheelchair users, taking a bath or shower requires some careful planning and preparation to ensure safety and comfort.

Here is a checklist of things you need to do before giving your loved one a bath or shower:

- Prepare everything you need in advance so you won't have to leave your loved one alone in the bathroom. Make sure everything – soap, shampoo, towels – is within easy reach.

- Place non-skid mats in the bath or shower, and check that the floor is not wet or slippery.

- After running the bath, remember to check its temperature. Put your elbow in the water. If you can't say the difference between hot or cold, then the water is at the right temperature.

- Ensure the room is comfortably warm.

Help your loved one get into the bathtub. For this you may need a mobility device, such as a bath lift. Whichever the means, don't hurry through the task. Always encourage the person being bathed to hold onto grab bars if your bathroom has them.

Remember, your aim is to make things easier so that your loved one can do as much as possible by themselves. This is very important – the more they practise their remaining skills, the higher the chances they can maintain independence and enjoy a normal life.

> **Tip**
>
> Use non-rinse soap. It is more practical to use and helps prevent skin breakdown.

Grooming – bed-bound people

If your loved one is bed-bound, you need to consider alternatives to bathing, like washing them in bed using a sponge and a non-rinse soap. You could also give them a bag bath or a towel bath.

Bag bath

- Place several washcloths into a plastic bag.
- Add warm water and a liquid, non-rinse soap. There should be just enough water to moisten the washcloths without soaking them.
- Wrap your loved one with a large towel or a blanket.
- Uncover just one body part, for example the shoulders, and massage them gently using one of the washcloths from the bag.
- Allow to air dry for a minute.
- Cover and do the same for every body part. Use the different washcloths for different body areas.

Towel bath

- Cover your loved one completely with a moist, warm bath towel.
- Apply a non-rinse soap to their skin.

'Remember, your aim is to make things easier so that your loved one can do as much as possible by themselves.'

■ Gently massage their skin through the towel.

Preventing and managing pressure ulcers

Wheelchair users and those who spend lot of time in bed are unable to change their position regularly. This puts them at risk of developing pressure ulcers – also called pressure sores or bedsores.

What are pressure ulcers?

Pressure ulcers are areas of broken skin that develop in the tailbone, hips or heels. They are caused when the skin and underlying tissues are compressed for prolonged periods of time between the bones and other hard surfaces, like a mattress or chair. The pressure exerted over the skin prevents blood from reaching the affected area. As a result, tissues and muscles do not receive enough oxygen and nutrients, and start to degenerate. This is accompanied by discomfort and pain.

Who is most at risk?

The risk that your loved one will develop a pressure ulcer increases if they:

■ Are older than 65, especially if they have a dementia illness like Alzheimer's disease. It has been estimated that of all individuals with pressure ulcers, approximately 70% are aged 70 years or over.

■ Have incontinence – in at-risk body areas, excessive moisture and substances in faeces and urine can irritate the skin, resulting in broken or otherwise damaged skin turning into a pressure ulcer. People with incontinence have a five-fold increased risk of developing a pressure ulcer.

■ Suffer from diabetes – reduced sensation caused by blood circulation problems that usually accompany this condition means that the sufferer may not be aware of skin breakdown, which could thus remain untreated and progress to pressure ulcers.

- Have had a pressure ulcer before – even if it healed well, skin and underlying tissues in areas where wounds were located are weak and, therefore, particularly vulnerable to breakdown.

If your loved one falls into one of these groups, you need to be particularly alert to the possibility that they may develop pressure ulcers. You should start implementing strategies immediately to prevent this from happening.

Promptness is vital because damaged skin areas can become pressure ulcers fairly quickly – people at risk can develop one in as little as two hours from pressure onset. The earlier you spot an ulcer, the higher the chances of a rapid and full recovery.

So, what can help reduce your loved one's likelihood of developing a pressure ulcer? According to guidelines from the National Institute for Clinical Excellence (NICE), effective prevention involves the implementation of the following strategies:

- Regular skin monitoring.

- Repositioning.

- Use of support surfaces.

- Incontinence management.

Skin monitoring

Check your loved one's skin regularly. You should do this twice daily (morning and night), or at least once daily. Inspect all of the body, particularly the shoulders, hips, base of the spine, bottom, ankles and heels. Look for changes that may indicate tissue damage, such as:

- Red and/or warm skin.

- Blisters.

- Tears.

- Bruises.

- Swelling.

- Scaling.

Tip

Always wash your hands with warm water and soap before inspecting the skin. If there are infected wounds, try to avoid cross-contamination by checking the less infected areas first.

The non-blanching erythema test

'Always wash your hands with warm water and soap before inspecting the skin. If there are infected wounds, try to avoid cross-contamination by checking the less infected areas first.'

Pay particular attention to dark skin areas surrounded by redness, as these can be a sign that deep tissue damage is occurring.

Note that sometimes areas of skin injury appear normal. It is generally easier to identify these areas with the use of the non-blanching erythema test:

- Place your finger on the suspected skin area. Apply a light pressure.
- If the skin turns white soon after you release the pressure, there is no damage that may lead to a pressure ulcer in that area.
- If the skin does not become white, damage is likely. Make sure your loved one sees a specialist as soon as possible.

Before you start inspecting your loved one's skin, ask their permission and make certain you have taken all the necessary steps to ensure dignity. Respect their need for privacy – keep the door closed and expose only one body area at a time. Provide a comfortable environment by ensuring the room is neither too hot nor cold.

If ulcers are present

If your loved one has pressure ulcers, you need to check these as well. You must tell the GP about any change. This will help establish whether or not the wound is healing.

Here is a checklist of things you should pay special attention to:

- The wound becoming wider.
- The wound becoming deeper.

- A bad odour coming from the wound.

- The area surrounding the wound is darkening, or unusually hot.

- There is pain and swelling.

Any of the above may indicate the presence of infection, in which case the person needs immediate medical attention. You can reduce the risk of infection by washing the wounds with soap and water or saline solution at each dressing, if instructed by your GP. Make sure the dressing does not exert pressure on the injury. To avoid further damage, it is also important not to remove it too frequently.

Different types of dressings can be more or less helpful. For example, some experts discourage the use of wet-to-dry dressings because these have been associated with increased pain and bleeding. Moist dressings, on the other hand, seem to be more effective at promoting healing. Whichever type you are going to use, make sure its adhesive parts are placed well outside the wound.

Repositioning

Repositioning helps prevent ulcers by reducing the pressure exerted on at-risk skin areas. You should change your loved one's position throughout the day – at least every two hours.

Tip

Never raise the head of the bed to 30° or more. Doing so increases the pressure on the tailbone and the lower back, in turn increasing the risk of developing new ulcers, or worsening old ones.

When repositioning, remember the following:

- To avoid further skin irritation and injury, always lift the person, don't drag them. For this you may want to use turning sheets. These are about half the length of normal sheets, and are placed under the person's body, from their head to their buttocks. Two carers can then grab the sheet's corners and move the person up and down without dragging them.

'Repositioning helps prevent ulcers by reducing the pressure exerted on at-risk skin areas. You should change your loved one's position throughout the day – at least every two hours.'

- Never place them on an ulcer or on their hips.

- Foster independence: if your loved one can change position by themselves, let them do so.

- If your loved one is in a wheelchair, encourage them to shift their weight (e.g. leaning forward or side-to-side) and to lift their bottom every 15 minutes or so.

- After repositioning a person in a wheelchair, always make sure they sit correctly. Their back should be flat with the head up, and their knees should be slightly lower than the hips. This will help avoid exerting pressure on the bottom and the hips.

Menna Lloyd Jones, a senior nurse tissue viability at North West Wales, also recommends: 'Give special attention to getting patients in and out of the wheelchair, making sure that they do not knock their arms or legs against sharp objects and, where possible, make sure that sharp edges are well padded. The same applies to getting them in and out of cars.'

Support surfaces

The strength and time of the pressure put on vulnerable areas can be reduced substantially with the use of support surfaces. These are also referred to as pressure relief equipment.

For example, if your loved one is confined to bed, they can use pillows or foam wedges. These can be placed under the calves to raise the feet off the bed, or they can be placed between the ankles or the knees to prevent them from touching each other.

Mattress overlays, foam mattresses, air-fluidised beds and heel and elbow protectors can also be used. Doughnut-shaped cushions are no longer recommended. Although they help relieve the pressure on the ulcer, they cut the blood flow to the area surrounding the ulcer, causing its deterioration. If your loved one is a wheelchair user, other support surfaces like pads and cushions are available. Your GP or nurse will give you advice on which one is best.

Managing incontinence

If your loved one has incontinence, try to anticipate their need to go to the bathroom, and clean them immediately if accidents occur. Use a mild soap and a soft sponge. Don't scrub the skin, and pat it gently when drying. Apply a moisturiser, if recommended by the GP. (See also chapter 9 for detailed information on how to deal with incontinence.)

Nutrition

Nutrition is an often overlooked aspect of pressure ulcer prevention and management, and yet it is one of the most crucial. Not eating and drinking enough can lead to weight loss and dehydration, both of which increase dramatically the risk of developing pressure ulcers. They also reduce the chances of a wound healing and, consequently, the likelihood of a full recovery. The general advice is to ensure that the person in your care eats a balanced diet and drinks plenty of fluids.

'Nutrition is an often overlooked aspect of pressure ulcer prevention and management, and yet it is one of the most crucial.'

Safe moving and lifting

> **Tip**
>
> If you feel weak, tired or ill, avoid moving your loved one. Ask someone else in the family to do it for you. In fact, having someone available to help with these tasks during the day is a good idea. It doesn't have to be the same person every time, but they should be more or less the same height as you, as this makes the job easier.

As a carer, you will assist your loved one with moving and lifting many times during the course of one day with changing position, getting in and out of bed and transferring from the chair to the bed, bathtub or toilet seat. So, you need to know how to do it safely.

Here is a list of key recommendations for moving and lifting your loved one without putting them, and yourself, at risk of injury.

- Before moving or lifting your loved one, make sure there are no obstacles on the floor. Also, if you wear jewellery, consider removing it as this may cause harm to the patient.

- Always encourage your loved one to help themselves. It will contribute to their sense of independence and self-confidence. However, remember not to rush them.

- Be certain your feet are stable on the floor, so as to avoid slipping.

- Maintain a correct posture throughout the task. Remind yourself to stand and sit up straight, and don't twist to the side. When bending, bend your knees and not the waist.

- Ensure every lifting movement is performed in a steady manner, and breathe regularly.

- Always lift the person. If you drag them, you may damage their skin.

- Should you feel pain when attempting to lift or move the person, don't carry on.

Equipment and adaptations

'There are many items that can make a big difference to the life of a person with a disability, allowing for greater independence and improved quality of life.'

There are many items that can make a big difference to the life of a person with a disability, allowing for greater independence and improved quality of life. These include adapted kitchen tools, mobility devices, modified furniture, bath boards, raised toilet seats, adjustable beds and stair lifts. A wide range of products are available for purchase from shops across the country. Remember that VAT is not charged on some of these items. Also, social services provide equipment for disabled people, so you may want to approach them and ask for information on what your loved one is entitled to have.

Furthermore, life can be much easier if your house has been adapted to facilitate the movements of the person in your care. Most common alterations include:

- Installing ramps.

- Placing grab bars and hand rails.

- Widening doors.

- Adjusting the height of light switches, mirrors and sinks.

Your local council may be able to help you meet the costs of house adaptations with a Disabled Facilities Grant, so that your loved one can continue to live there.

Receiving the grant doesn't affect other benefits your loved one receives – and if they are a tenant, the landlord can claim the grant on their behalf. The amount of money paid varies depending on your, or your loved one's, income and can be no higher than about £30,000. To apply for a Disabled Facilities Grant, you need to contact your local council. If you are entitled, the money will be paid either to you or the company that will carry out the alterations. Depending on the circumstances, this may be before any work starts or on job completion.

Dealing with depression

Your loved one may struggle to adjust to life with a disability, especially if this is the result of a sudden event (such as an accident or fall) or an acute medical problem (like a stroke). Initially, there will be a sense of disbelief, and then great anger and frustration as they realise that their life will be different. These feelings will turn into sadness, which may put your loved one at risk of depression.

Who is at risk?

Some factors increase the likelihood of developing depression. Look at the list below and see which ones apply to your loved one.

- Past episodes of depression.
- A family history of the condition.
- Recent negative life events (e.g. the death of a partner).
- A mental illness (e.g. dementia).
- Blindness and/or deafness.
- A chronic condition (e.g. arthritis, diabetes or heart disease).

'Your loved one may struggle to adjust to life with a disability, especially if this is the result of a sudden event (such as an accident or fall) or an acute medical problem (like a stroke).

If any of these factors are present, you need to be particularly watchful for signs and symptoms of depression, because the earlier you spot them, the higher the chances of a full recovery. You should look for:

- Loss of interest in activities they previously enjoyed.
- Persistent sadness.
- Crying for no apparent reason.
- Significant weight loss or gain.
- Unexplained fatigue.
- Sleeping too much or too little.
- Social isolation.
- Feelings of hopelessness and guilt.
- Attention problems.
- Talking about life not being worth living.

'Encourage the person in your care to talk. Show understanding for their feelings and don't dismiss any of their worries as unimportant.'

What about treatment?

Medication is likely to be prescribed if the depression is severe. However, medication is not recommended if the patient is suffering from mild to moderate depression. In this case, the first line of treatment consists of providing the person with practical and emotional support to facilitate their recovery. Researchers at the University of North Carolina at Charlotte (Flood and Buckwalter, 2009), in the US, recommend the following:

- Encourage the person in your care to talk. Show understanding for their feelings and don't dismiss any of their worries as unimportant.
- Provide daily opportunities for engagement in activities they like.
- Help them to maintain and develop their network of friends.
- Make sure they exercise regularly, eat healthy and get enough sleep.

Out and about in a wheelchair

Some of the strategies listed opposite imply that the patient can still get out and about, just like it was before the disability. For those who are confined to a bed, this can be difficult, but not impossible. You will just need to bring the outside world to them, rather than taking them outside.

Some ideas you can help your loved one with could include:

* Placing the bed in such a way that they can enjoy the view from the window.

* Organising visits from friends and relatives.

* Seeing if they can use a computer for emailing and social networking.

* Providing opportunities for engagement in activities they can do in bed (e.g. listening to music, reading and board games).

* Keeping them informed by ensuring access to TV, radio and newspapers.

'In warm weather, make sure your loved one wears light clothing, a hat and sunscreen.'

Case study

'After the accident, my mum has become withdrawn and really sad. She doesn't talk much. She doesn't want to go anywhere – she doesn't want to be seen in her wheelchair. She used to love walking by the sea. So, we brought her on the promenade on Sunday for a walk along the seafront. She smiled for the first time in months.'

William, age 39.

Things are easier, of course, if your loved one is a wheelchair user. Going out with them is not difficult or expensive to accomplish. You just need to follow a few simple recommendations to ensure your trips outdoors are safe and pleasant.

* In warm weather, make sure your loved one wears light clothing, a hat and sunscreen. Offer them plenty to drink and check in advance that there is a shaded area available. Also, consider that some wheelchairs are made of materials that become extremely hot if left under direct sunlight for too long.

- In cold weather, ensure that they are well dressed. Remember that wheelchair users cannot keep themselves warm by walking and moving like most of us do.

- If it is raining, an umbrella will not help protect your loved one from cars splashing and puddles. Ensure they wear waterproof clothing that covers them completely, including the legs and feet. Choose items that can be put on easily without leaving the wheelchair and always carry them with you.

- When planning visits to theatres, cinemas, restaurants, museums, historic buildings, galleries, parks and other places of leisure or interest, check the websites to make sure they are accessible to wheelchairs, and whether they provide any special equipment or assistance.

- If you will be travelling by train, consider buying a Disabled Persons Railcard. It costs £18 for one year or £48 for three years, and allows you and the person in your care to obtain one-third off most rail fares in the UK (see help list).

- Consider taking a holiday. Many organisations throughout the UK offer group holidays as well as outdoor activities specifically designed for disabled people, their family and friends.

Tip

Are you planning to push your loved one in a wheelchair for some time? If so, consider wearing a pair of padded gloves, such as those worn by cyclists, to prevent your hands from getting sore.

Other disabilities

Physical disabilities do not always entail being confined to a bed or wheelchair. Due to mobility impairments, they can cause a range of other problems. For example, some people have impaired functioning in everyday activities because they cannot use their hands, as a result of a medical condition or following an accident. Vision or hearing loss is another example. These are dealt with in the next chapter. Other common types of physical disability are listed in the table below, which also lists strategies for making tasks easier.

Disability	Strategies
One arm/hand.	Many simple tasks can still be performed after clamping or taping firmly to the table the object that should be handled with the missing limb.
Inability to move fingers, hands and wrists due to chronic conditions, such as arthritis and osteoporosis.	Use the hand-on-hand technique. Place your hand over the patient's hand and guide them through the task they need to perform.
Hand tremor; for example, suffered by those with essential tremor or Parkinson's disease.	Find weighted, large-bodied tools, utensils, pens, cutlery and so on to improve hand steadiness. Also, place items such as plates on a rubber mat or damp cloth to avoid sliding.
Extreme hand weakness.	Provide lighter than normal tools, utensils, cutlery and other objects.

Summing Up

There is often a misconception that people with a physical disability can no longer live a normal life. Not true. With your help, a disabled person can have a happy and fulfilling life, just like everybody else.

- Encourage regular exercise in any form that best suits your loved one, according to their remaining abilities, health status and their GP's advice.

- Take steps to ensure bathing/showering is safe and pleasant. Consider towel or bag bath alternatives for those confined to their bed.

- Prevent and manage pressure ulcers effectively: monitor the person's skin twice a day, reposition at least every two hours, use pressure-relief equipment, address incontinence and ensure adequate food and fluids are consumed.

- Follow the recommendations for safe moving and lifting.

- Make everyday life easier with equipment like mobility devices and adapted kitchen tools, and home adaptations such as ramps, grab bars and wide door openings.

- Learn how to recognise, prevent and address depression in your loved one. Keep them socially and physically active.

Chapter Seven

Caring for People with Sensory Impairments

Eyesight and hearing loss are a relatively common problem among adults. According to a report published in 2008 by the NHS, about 300,000 people in England are registered as blind or partially sighted. More than 60% are 75 years or older, and approximately 30% also have another physical or mental disability.

The situation is even worse for hearing loss. RNID estimates that there are approximately nine million deaf or hard-of-hearing people in the UK. Of these, the majority are adults over the age of 65. About 23,000 deaf people are also blind.

The first part of this chapter describes how to care for a blind or partially sighted loved one. The second part looks at how to assist someone with deafness or partial hearing loss. You will find step-by-step, practical guidance on how to make communication easier and life still enjoyable, as well as information on where to find help.

Partially sighted and blind people

People develop eyesight problems for various reasons. In the UK, the most common causes of partial or complete blindness are age-related conditions, such as:

- Glaucoma – in glaucoma the optic nerve is damaged because of too much pressure inside the eye, which causes progressive loss of peripheral vision.

- Macular degeneration – the macula (the central part of the retina inside the back of the eye) is affected, which leads to the loss of central vision.

Why communication is important

Although different eye diseases affect a person's vision in different ways, all of them impair, at least to a certain extent, their ability to communicate with others. This increases dramatically their risk of becoming lonely and isolated and makes them vulnerable to depression.

Work conducted by Australian psychologists Karen Berman and Henry Brodaty shows that eye diseases, like macular degeneration, are also associated with increased anxiety, emotional distress and a high risk of early death. So, keeping communication going is of paramount importance, and for this you need to know how to interact with the person correctly.

'Probably one of the most important things you can do for your loved one, in terms of communication, is to be descriptive when talking.'

- Always approach your loved one slowly to avoid startling them. If you need to go into another room, don't do so without saying you are leaving.

- Attract their attention with a light touch on their arm before speaking.

- Place yourself in a good light and always in front of them. Many blind people can still recognise a shape if it's close enough and well lit.

- Speak clearly in a calm tone of voice, and don't be loud. The fact that your loved one can't see you well doesn't mean they can't hear you.

You can be their eyes

Probably one of the most important things you can do for your loved one, in terms of communication, is to be descriptive when talking. This means using plenty of adjectives so that they can visualise the things you refer to, even if they can't see them. In fact, they can see most things through your eyes. You just need to remember to bring light, shapes and colours back into their life by describing what you see around you. Any of the things you tell your loved one about – the weather, the view from a window, objects, animals and people – will make their days brighter.

Guiding your loved one

The technique mentioned in the previous section is also useful when you are guiding your loved one to warn them about any potential hazards and to help them go in the right direction. Also, you should remember:

- Have them take you by the arm, not vice versa.

- Be specific when mentioning obstacles and say where they are. For steps, you should also say whether they go up or down.

- If your loved one wants to sit down, gently place their hand on the back of the chair so they can orientate themselves.

Life goes on

One of the most effective ways for coping with life-changing conditions like blindness is to maintain a can-do attitude. There is no reason why your loved one should stop doing the things they used to enjoy. They just need to find new ways of doing them. And thanks to modern technology, this is possible for many activities. Here are a few examples:

- Audio CDs can help people continue to 'read' books. The RNIB distributes audio books, or talking books, to its members (see help list).

- Audio description services are available which allow a blind person to enjoy the cinema, the theatre and TV programmes by telling the listener what is happening when there is no dialogue.

- There is also a wide range of games, including board games, crosswords and puzzles, specifically for use by blind or partially sighted people, as well as art supplies if your loved one enjoys painting or drawing.

- Most types of sports are also possible – from football and cricket to tennis and archery, to name just a few. Running and swimming can also be continued, as long as the person is accompanied by a sighted companion.

Making things easier outdoors...

Another popular leisure activity that the vast majority of blind or partially sighted people can continue to enjoy is walking. They can do this independently, with the help of canes or guide dogs, or accompanied by another person, whether it is walking in the park, visiting a friend or going to a local shop.

- Remind your loved one to ask for help if unsure about when and where it is safe to cross a road.

- If they have a guide dog, encourage them to remind the people they meet that they should not distract the dog in any way, because this can lower his or her concentration.

- Check in advance to ensure that new routes are accessible to a blind person. In this regard, consider that for a visually impaired person, going downhill is more difficult than going uphill.

If your loved one enjoys country walks, you may want to check out organisations like Ramblers and the RNIB. They offer programmes of country walks for blind and visually impaired people throughout the UK and Ireland. These are invaluable opportunities for your loved one to exercise, enjoy some fresh air and make new friends.

... And indoors

Tip

Keep utensils, tools, clothes and accessories that have a similar use, or are used together, in the same place.

At home, adopt a number of simple strategies to help your loved one get around as safely and independently as possible.

- Always keep objects and furniture in the same place. This enables the person to memorise where things are located.

- Eliminate worn carpets and rugs, as well as loose electrical cords, to reduce the risk of falls. For the same reason, you should never leave doors – including cabinet and closet doors – half open. Also, encourage your loved one to use handrails on stairs.

- Make sure all rooms are well lit.

- Make the most of colour contrast to make it easier to see things, like doorknobs, light switches, dinnerware and towels. Choose colours that contrast sharply with doors, walls, tablecloths and bathroom tiles, respectively.

- Use Braille-embossed, or large-print, adhesive labels on drawers, cabinets and containers, including food cans and boxes.

- Make sure that all mats are non-skid in the bathroom.

- Replace white toilet seats with dark ones.

Tip

Set the table always in the same way so that your loved can find everything they need without help.

A few more general tips include:

- At mealtimes, make sure there is good light straight above the table.

- If your loved one enjoys cooking, make sure they wear short sleeves when working at the hob and use oven gloves to remove pans from it.

- When using water, remind them to open the cold tap first and then the hot one to avoid scalding themselves.

- Consider that striped or coloured toothpastes are easier to see than white ones.

- Look for everyday objects (clocks, CD players, mobile phones) that are adapted for blind or partially sighted people. RNIB has more than 1,000 of these products (see help list).

'Eliminate worn carpets and rugs, as well as loose electrical cords, to reduce the risk of falls. For the same reason, you should never leave doors – including cabinet and closet doors – half open. Also, encourage your loved one to use handrails on stairs.'

Reading and writing

There are also several steps you can take to make it possible for your loved one to continue to read and write. These vary depending on the severity and type of eyesight problem, so you should talk with your GP first about which intervention is the most appropriate. As mentioned earlier, audio and talking books are one option. Other examples of things that can help include the following:

- Ask your loved one to consider learning the Braille technique.
- Provide large-print reading material.
- Encourage the use of low-vision devices, such as magnifying lenses.
- Consider buying a computer screen magnification programme.
- Read novels, newspapers and magazines to them.

Canes

The majority of visually impaired people in the UK find it easier to get around with the help of a cane. This is no ordinary cane, but a proper mobility tool, and as such it requires training in order to be used safely and effectively. A white cane (also called a guide cane) allows the user to identify and negotiate obstacles. Thus, it gives considerable freedom and independence.

'Sometimes blind people carry a shorter, collapsible cane. This is called a 'symbol' cane and serves only to indicate that the person has sight problems; it is not a mobility tool. Symbol canes with red bands on them indicate that the person is both blind and deaf.

Guide dogs

A smaller proportion of blind or partially sighted people use a guide dog. If your loved one does not have a guide dog but you think they may need one, you can find relevant information from the Guide Dogs for the Blind Association. This is the organisation responsible for providing training to guide dog users in the UK (see help list).

'Sometimes blind people carry a shorter, collapsible cane. This is called a "symbol" cane and serves only to indicate that the person has sight problems; it is not a mobility tool. Symbol canes with red bands on them indicate that the person is both blind and deaf.'

Case study

'My sister has been blind from birth. When she started high school, six months ago, mum used to walk her to the college down the road. My sister found it really embarrassing, so dad came up with an idea: a guide dog! My sister now walks to college by herself. In fact, she never misses an opportunity to walk! She is much happier and has many more friends.'

Lucy, aged 13.

Support groups

To help promote friendships, socialising and a fulfilling life, encourage your loved one to join a support group. 'It is advantageous to put patients in touch with support groups such as the AMD Alliance and the RNIB', says Sue Watkinson, a lecturer at Thames Valley University. 'The Macular Disease Society also offers essential help and support in meeting a variety of needs and setting up patient support groups in hospital eye units.'

Deaf and hard-of-hearing individuals

In about 90% of cases, deafness is the result of problems in the tiny hair cells that transmit sound in the inner ear. This type of deafness is called sensorineural hearing loss. It can be caused by infections, certain medications (like antibiotics), prolonged exposure to excessive loud noise or old age, and is not reversible.

Fewer cases of deafness are caused by problems with the eardrum or the three tiny bones in the middle ear. This is called conductive hearing loss and is reversible in most patients.

Like eyesight problems, hearing loss can limit considerably a person's ability to communicate with other people. In addition, research shows that everyday skills like walking, dressing, eating and even cognition are affected. According to findings by researchers at the University of Brandeis in Massachusetts, negative effects on cognition are due to the fact that in order to be able to

'Like eyesight problems, hearing loss can limit considerably a person's ability to communicate with other people.'

understand what other people say, deaf or hard-of-hearing individuals use up mental faculties that would otherwise be available for other cognitive tasks, like memory (Wingfield et al., 2005).

Keeping the communication going

It is important that you adopt strategies that facilitate communication with the person with hearing loss. This ensures you can understand and meet their needs. It also enables them to continue to fully participate in activities with other people and, therefore, avoid isolation and depression.

Tip

When approaching a deaf person, lightly tap on their shoulder or arm. You will get their attention without startling them. If you are entering a room the person is in, switch the lights on and off a few times. A gentle waving of the hand will also do.

Here are some important points for you to remember:

- Eliminate excessive background noise. Consider that carpet, rugs and thick wallpaper make rooms less noisy.

- Encourage family and friends to sit near your loved one when they talk with them.

- At mealtimes, make sure the seating arrangement allows your loved one to see everyone's face.

- Face your loved one during a conversation, and speak clearly.

- Do a practical demonstration of tasks you would like your loved one to do.

Sign language

In addition to the strategies above, you and your loved one may want to learn new methods of communicating that rely on gestures and expressions rather than words. One of these methods is sign language. This is a language in its own right, so it has different grammar and rules than English. There are also different sign languages for different countries. Most people with hearing loss in the UK use British Sign Language (BSL), although some people prefer to use American Sign Language. There are free BSL resources at www.british-sign.co.uk.

Lip-reading tips

The most commonly used communication method after sign language is lip reading. Of course, this is not a language in its own right, as it only helps the deaf or hard of hearing understand others. However, it can greatly improve the conversation if the person speaking knows how to make it easier for the lip reader to understand their words.

If you want to use lip reading with your loved one, follow these tips:

- Make sure they can see you well.

- Before you start speaking, wait for them to concentrate on your lips, otherwise they may miss some words and this may prevent them from understanding the rest of the conversation.

- Speak slowly and open your mouth widely when speaking, so as to shape the words well with your lips.

- Don't shout.

- Don't talk with food in your mouth.

- Use facial expression and gesture to support the meaning of your words.

Hearing aids

Hearing aids are of great benefit because they help the wearer understand others. As a result, conversation becomes easier and the person's self-confidence improves.

Hearing aids amplify and improve the quality of the sound, while reducing background noise. Older analogue ones are being replaced by digital aids; these come in many forms and sizes and can be worn inside or behind the ear.

The NHS provides free digital, behind-the-ear hearing aids to all patients with hearing loss. If you think your loved one could benefit from wearing hearing aids, visit their GP together. He or she will refer them to an NHS audiologist, who will carry out some tests to decide whether they are needed. NHS hearing aids last approximately five years. All spare parts and repairs are free of charge.

If the person in your care does wear hearing aids, you need to make sure you both know how to take care of them. If you are not certain, ask the audiologist. It is a good idea to write down important instructions so you will not forget anything crucial that needs to be done.

Here are some important reminders:

'If the person in your care does wear hearing aids, you need to make sure you both know how to take care of them. If you are not certain, ask the audiologist.'

- Excessive moisture and heat can cause damage to hearing aids, so they should not be used while showering or using a hair dryer.

- Remove the batteries when the hearing aids are not being used.

- Cleaning should always be done according to the manufacturer's instructions, usually with a soft, dry cloth.

- Remove any wax that may be covering the ear moulds.

- Encourage your loved one to lean over a table when inserting or removing their hearing aids. This will prevent them from falling on the floor if they're dropped.

Tip

With your loved one, decide on a place to keep their hearing aids when they are not wearing them, and don't change it. This will reduce the chance that they might be misplaced.

If your loved one attends groups or a day care centre, labels can prevent their hearing aids from being lost, should they need to be removed for any reason.

Here is a quick checklist of things to do when inserting hearing aids.

- Check that the batteries are fully charged.

- Make sure the hearing aids are inserted properly, and in the correct ears. If your loved one wears two hearing aids, it may be helpful to label each device with the words 'left' and 'right'.

- Ensure all hearings aids are switched on.

- Set the volume at a comfortable level.

Cochlear implants

Hearing aids are not effective for everyone. Certain forms of hearing loss may be resolved, although never completely, with electronic devices called cochlear implants. These consist of a small sound processor, which is surgically implanted under the skin behind the ear, and a tiny microphone with antenna, worn in the outer ear. The microphone receives the sound, which is converted to electrical signals and sent to the processor and then to the brain.

People who may benefit from a cochlear implant include children and adults who are deaf in both ears. Cochlear implantation is performed under general anaesthetic and requires up to a few days stay in hospital. The external part of the device will be placed about a month after surgery.

Many people who receive a cochlear implant find it easier to understand others. This is commonly reported as the greatest benefit of a cochlear implant. However, sounds are different from how the person remembers them. For this reason, after the surgery all patients need to re-learn how to hear. The training is usually done by audiologists and speech therapists.

'Many people who receive a cochlear implant find it easier to understand others. This is commonly reported as the greatest benefit of a cochlear implant.'

Making things happen... anyway!

Hearing loss and deafness is often associated with feelings of being cut off and isolated, which may lead to depression. Ensuring good communication is important to prevent this from happening, but it is not enough. As a carer, you also need to take steps to facilitate your loved one's successful participation in activities, so that they can continue to enjoy doing the things they like.

Here are some ideas:

- Have a book at hand for writing down instructions when needed. This way, it will be easier for your loved one to understand.

- Use pictures to demonstrate tasks or instructions.

- Make sure that TV programmes and DVDs have subtitles.

- Remind people who participate in activities with your loved one to use the communication strategies described earlier.

Hearing dogs

There is an additional effective way to make the life of a deaf or hard-of-hearing person easier. The charity Hearing Dogs for Deaf People (see help list) trains dogs to alert their owners to everyday household sounds, like telephones, alarm clocks, smoke detectors, oven timers and more. This results in greater independence and safety.

Summing Up

Although your loved one can be profoundly affected by partial or complete hearing or vision loss, they can still lead normal and enjoyable lives.

- Learn strategies that will help keep the communication open with your loved one.

- Ensure they make the most of aids and assistive devices available to them.

- Implement changes that make it easier and safer to get around the home.

- Help your loved one to do as much as they can on their own, so as to foster their independence.

- Take active steps to ensure their full participation in leisure and social activities.

For more information see *Deafness and Hearing Loss – The Essential Guide* and *Sight Loss – The Essential Guide* (Need2Know).

Chapter Eight

Caring for Dementia Patients and the Mentally Ill

A characteristic feature of many mental illnesses is a reduced ability to communicate and interact with other people. This can have serious consequences for both patients and their carers. Researchers at the University of Western Ontario in Canada have found, for example, that the inability to interact with others leads affected patients to become frustrated, anxious and, in some cases, even aggressive (Savundranayagam et al., 2005).

This has a harmful impact on their carers, who end up experiencing high levels of stress on a regular basis and become vulnerable to depression and burnout. You, therefore, need to be familiar with practical ways to overcome communication problems and make interaction possible.

Of course, the loss of a patient's ability to communicate is more or less severe depending on how far into the disease or condition the person is, which is why, as the illness progresses, you will need to adopt different strategies to keep communication flowing.

This chapter will guide you through a number of interventions purposely developed by researchers for carers of people with a mental illness. You will find how you can use these strategies to ensure that you and your loved one continue to enjoy a meaningful and satisfying life.

Appropriate approach

First, you need to know how to approach your loved one in the most appropriate way. In patients with impaired cognition, the ability to relate to their environment is not the same as in cognitively healthy people. In other words, they don't fully understand what happens around them. This means that they don't react to people, objects and situations the way most of us normally do.

For example, if you make a sudden movement, a person with dementia may think you want to hit them and may try to hit you back, and the same goes if you approach them from behind. What is the best way to prevent these reactions? You need to keep in mind a few simple, yet effective, recommendations:

'In patients with impaired cognition, the ability to relate to their environment is not the same as in healthy people.'

- Avoid approaching your loved one from behind.
- Move slowly towards them.
- Avoid sudden movements of the arms and hands.
- If they are sitting, don't lean towards them. Rather, kneel down to their level.
- Make eye contact before speaking.
- Always ask permission before touching them.

Communication

Normally, people with impaired cognition become progressively unable to understand and be understood. This happens in people with dementia. With time they start to:

- Use wrong or non-existent words.
- Talk at the wrong time during a conversation.
- Speak too much and too loudly.
- Repeat the same sentence many times.
- Change the subject of the conversation inappropriately.

Avoid embarrassment

Tip

If your loved one doesn't understand, repeat things exactly as you have said them. Use the same words and sentences. Avoid rephrasing, as experts say this tends to increase confusion in the person with cognitive impairment.

Initially, the major problem is that patients tend to avoid engaging in conversation because they fear making mistakes. They still retain much of their cognition and, therefore, are well aware of what they say. They know if they skip a word, make one up or lose their train of thought, so they simply stop talking to avoid embarrassment and frustration. This is precisely what you should focus on. Don't say anything that could provoke these feelings, or make them worse.

For example:

- Avoid pointing out mistakes.

- Refrain from saying things like: 'You forgot that again!' or 'Don't you remember?'

- Give gentle reminders only if needed, and always with tact and discretion.

Helpful strategies

Tip

Ask questions with a 'yes' or 'no' answer, and be specific. Avoid saying: 'Would you like something to eat?' Rather, say: 'Would you like a slice of cake?' Give your loved one all the time they need to respond (this may take several minutes, in some cases) without showing irritation or distracting your attention away from them.

At some point, the language skills of your loved one will be severely affected and you will need to find new ways of communicating. The strategies highlighted below have been developed over the years by researchers specifically for dementia carers:

- Eliminate background noise: switch the TV or radio off, and close doors or windows as necessary.

- Get your loved one's attention before speaking, and look them in the eyes while talking.

- Use short, simple sentences with words that are familiar to your loved one.

- Make sure you show reassurance and love when talking – use a soft and pleasant tone of voice.

- Listen to them without interrupting, and show genuine interest in what they say. Lean forward and occasionally nod your head in sign of approval.

- Check that your loved one has understood what you've said. Repeat things as many times as necessary.

- Limit choices to two or three items: 'Would you like to wear the red jumper or the blue jumper?'

Don't give up

Patients with severe cognitive impairment lose almost completely their ability to talk. At this point, communication mostly relies on the senses. Words alone are no longer enough to communicate with the person in your care. Once again, you need to find new strategies in addition to the ones described above. The key is in using different tones of voice, gestures and facial expressions to help your loved one understand what you say. For example:

- Use pictures or drawings to indicate a certain object, remind them of a particular event or to illustrate a task they need to perform. For instance, show them a picture of a toothbrush if you want to tell them to brush their teeth.

- Likewise, you may want to use the smell of freshly baked bread to help them know that lunch is ready; or the scent of their preferred soap to help them understand that it's bath time.

Remember, if your loved one is barely able to talk, their wellbeing depends completely on your ability to pick up cues from their behaviour. If their mood or tone of voice suddenly changes, or they consistently avoid looking you in the eyes, become restless, make fists, frown or clench their teeth, something is wrong. You need to find out what it is immediately. Studies show that these behaviours always have a meaning. They may be the person's reaction to pain, hunger, thirst or other unmet needs. So, by recognising and addressing them, you can save your loved one from needless suffering.

Care tips

Whether your loved one is having a meal, brushing their teeth or taking a bath, it is extremely important that you help them be as independent as possible. The benefits of doing so are twofold: not only will this approach improve the person's self-esteem and sense of satisfaction, it will reduce your workload too, in turn lowering your risk of stress and burnout.

In order to achieve this, tasks have to be constantly modified and tailored to the remaining skills of the person in your care. You need to continually monitor what your loved one can and cannot do and adapt tasks accordingly. Break them down into a sequence of one-step actions, and allow plenty of time to complete each step.

> 'Remember, if your loved one is barely able to talk, their wellbeing depends completely on your ability to pick up cues from their behaviour.'

Tip

If your loved one finds themselves stuck at some point while performing a certain task, or seems unable to start doing something, show them what to do; do the task yourself, first.

Let's see what this means in practice, with an example. If your loved one is in the advanced stages of Alzheimer's disease and you want them to wash their hands by themselves, you will increase the chances of them successfully doing so by giving them simple, one-step instructions:

- Please, open the tap.

- Now wet your hands under the tap.

- Take the soap.
- Rub your hands with the soap.
- Put the soap back.
- Rub your hands together.
- Rinse your hands under the tap.
- Take the towel.
- Dry your hands.
- Close the tap.

Meals

Of course, not all mental disorders affect a person's ability to function normally and perform everyday activities like eating, dressing, bathing and so on. However, some do, including dementia illnesses like Alzheimer's disease.

Basic strategies

Over time, eating and drinking become challenges for individuals with this condition. Most Alzheimer's disease patients cannot recognise food and what it is for, or even remember how to eat. Putting every possible effort in making mealtimes easier for your loved one is of paramount importance to prevent them from losing weight and reduce their risk of developing health problems associated with malnutrition. You can assist the person with dementia while still fostering their independence by using these simple, yet effective, basic strategies:

- Provide plenty of verbal prompts.
- Praise often, encourage and smile.
- Remind your loved one to eat one food item at a time.
- Offer finger food so that they can use their hands if they don't remember how to use knives, forks and spoons.

- Do things in advance that your loved one would find too difficult to do, such as opening milk cartons, buttering bread and cutting meat.
- Sit at the table and eat with them.

Create the right environment

Ensuring a calm and pleasant environment is also very important. Studies have found that minimising distractions at mealtimes is an effective way to help patients focus on eating. Conversation, music and good lighting are also helpful, while colour contrast between plates and the table can help them find food items more easily.

Bathing

This section focuses on what is probably one of the most stressful experiences facing carers of people with a mental illness like Alzheimer's disease: bathing or showering. When people with dementia try to make sense of a situation, they do it on the basis of what is left of their reasoning skills. Consequently, they understand situations in a distorted way. As a result, familiar tasks like taking a bath become frightening. The person doesn't understand what's happening to them, and could become combative or distressed.

Yet there are strategies that can make bathing easier and enjoyable. Dr Kevan Namazi, of the University of Texas Southwestern in the US, says the key is to meet the preferences of the person. So, your first step is to make sure you do things according to your loved one's likes and dislikes. For example, plan for them to take their bath/shower at the time of the day they prefer, using their favourite bathing items and routines.

Once you know your loved one's preferences, follow the recommendations given in chapter 6 on how to make bathing or showering easier.

'Ensuring a calm and pleasant environment is also very important.'

> **Tip**
>
> Protect your loved one's eyes with a cloth during hair washing. While showering, use the less powerful spray as it is less frightening.

If your loved one refuses to be bathed

In this case, you shouldn't force them. You will only increase their frustration and the likelihood that they become combative. Rather, try this:

- Distract them – talk about something they like, look together at a magazine or some pictures, make a little joke, offer them a favourite snack or drink, and then try again.

- Give them a reason for having a bath – for instance, a trip to the shops or tea with their best friend.

'Music also appears to be helpful at preventing agitation and promoting relaxation.'

When nothing helps

Simply schedule bathing for another time or consider alternatives, such as washing one body part every day. Other methods like the bag bath and the towel bath described in detail in chapter 6 are also very effective. The *Journal of the American Geriatrics Society*, for example, reports that in a study conducted by the University of North Carolina, towel baths reduced dementia-related aggressive outbursts during bathing by more than 50% (Sloane et al., 2004).

Music also appears be helpful at preventing agitation and promoting relaxation. Make sure you play your loved one's favourite songs though!

If the person becomes combative

We have seen that there is a lot you can do to give your loved one a pleasant bathing experience. This, however, does not eliminate the possibility of the person becoming aggressive. And, if that happens, you need to know what to do.

Stay calm and avoid arguing. Keep talking gently, even if your loved one yells, calls you names or threatens you. The key is to keep in mind that such behaviours are caused by the illness, so whatever the person says or does, don't take it personally; keep showing your affection and give them all your help and support. You need to reassure your loved one. Say something like, 'It's okay, don't be afraid, I am here to help you.'

You will find more advice on how to deal with combative behaviour in people with a mental disorder in the 'Common problems' section of this chapter.

Lastly, consider that it is normal for people with dementia to refuse to change their clothes after a bath or shower. If this happens, try replacing the dirty garments with the clean ones when they cannot see you. They may then put them on, without noticing that they have been changed.

Tip

If your loved one prefers to take showers, use hand-held devices. They can be used on one body area at the time – for this reason they are usually less frightening and better tolerated.

'A large part of helping your loved one with this problem is about knowing the right coping strategies.'

Dressing

Loss of cognition has a bad effect on the ability to perform almost any everyday grooming activity, including dressing. This is made even more difficult by the fact that, as the disease progresses, the person also loses their fine motor skills. Simple things like buttoning a shirt or fastening a zip become daunting tasks. Not only is the person no longer able to remember how to do things, they cannot actually do them.

A large part of helping your loved one with this problem is about knowing the right coping strategies. Here are a few examples:

- Lay your loved one's clothes on the bed in the exact order in which they have to be worn.

- Hand the clothes directly to them (in the order they need to be put on), if they cannot dress themselves.

- Tell your loved one what they need to do with each item. Remember, simplicity is key, so use short sentences of familiar words.

- Avoid saying things like, 'Put your right sock on, and then the left one.' People with severe cognitive impairment can no longer distinguish between left and right, and become confused, which in turn increases their frustration. Simply say: 'Put your sock on, and now the other one.'

- Be patient. Your loved one needs time to accomplish even the simplest task. Don't step in because you are in a rush. Give them plenty of time to finish what they are doing.

> ## Tip
>
> The following items can make dressing significantly easier:
>
> - Shirts and trousers with Velcro fastenings, rather than zips or buttons.
>
> - Sweatshirts and t-shirts with large neck openings.
>
> - Items with loose sleeves.

Oral care

'Ensuring good oral care is of particular importance because, compared to other people, patients with a mental illness like dementia have an increased risk of developing cavities and losing teeth, which puts them at risk of malnutrition.'

Ensuring good oral care is of particular importance because, compared to other people, patients with a mental illness like dementia have an increased risk of developing cavities and losing teeth, which puts them at risk of malnutrition. Furthermore, they are more likely to suffer from gum disease, oral infections, cardiovascular problems and pneumonia, according to recent studies.

Regular visits to the dentist are, of course, crucial but not enough. You should ensure your loved one brushes their teeth after each meal, for at least two minutes, using fluoridated toothpaste. Daily use of dental floss and mouth rinse is also recommended.

Where to start?

Once again, it is paramount that you find ways to make the task so simple that your loved one can do it successfully with minimum effort. For example:

- You may want to make the toothbrush easier to handle by wrapping it up with foam or bubble-wrap, or by attaching to it a bicycle handlebar or a tennis ball.
- Give them simple, one-step instructions.
- Brush your teeth together, and encourage your loved one to copy your movements.

Even if your loved one can brush their teeth independently, they will probably need help with flossing. However, make sure they can tolerate flossing before doing it. The same goes for electric toothbrushes, to which some people with dementia react with fear and combative behaviour.

If they can't brush their teeth

- Ask your loved one to sit on a dining chair.
- Stand behind them, and gently hold their head with one hand.
- With the other hand, brush their teeth.

Consider that people with dementia like routine. You may find it helpful to ensure that your loved one can brush their teeth every day at the same time.

Common problems

Dementia illnesses, such as Alzheimer's disease, are just one of several types of mental disorders. These include, among others, obsessive compulsive disorder, schizophrenia, bipolar disorder (also called manic depression, or more simply bipolar), depression and anxiety.

Each of these mental illnesses manifests itself in a very distinctive way; however, some share one or more symptoms. For example, mood swings are typical of depression and bipolar, and delusions and hallucinations can be found in dementia and schizophrenia.

Below is a list of the most common of these symptoms, together with the strategies that have proved to be effective at controlling them.

Mood swings

In people with certain mental illnesses, such as bipolar, mood swings are not like the highs and lows most of us experience. The person shifts very rapidly – within minutes or hours – from being extremely happy and excited, often for no real reason, to being deeply sad and depressed. You need to deal with the two different emotional states in different ways. When the person is in a low mood, you can help by listening to them and showing understanding of their feelings. Appropriate use of humour and distractions, such as taking a walk together, also help greatly.

When the person is in a state of euphoria, you need to focus on making sure that their energy and excitement don't escalate out of control. Seeing your loved one happy certainly is a refreshing sight, but don't add wood to the fire. Shift their attention away from situations that might increase the euphoria, such as animated conversations.

Remember that there is also a great deal you can do to reduce the severity and frequency of their mood swings. One of the most important is to ensure that your loved one does not stop taking their medication, unless instructed by their GP.

Tip

Have your loved one keep a stress ball, or another non-noisy object that they can squeeze, in their pocket. They will be able to quietly satisfy their need for fidgeting anytime they want, without disturbing other people.

Also:

- Provide your loved one with opportunities for regular exercise.
- Identify situations that might trigger changes in mood, and try to avoid them.

80

■ Encourage your loved one to practise relaxation techniques (see chapter 5), and to engage in activities they like.

Obsessions and compulsions

Obsessions are recurrent thoughts or beliefs – like fear of disease, contamination or excessive concerns about hygiene. They are a characteristic symptom of certain mental illnesses, such as obsessive compulsive disorder (OCD), and can cause high levels of anxiety and stress.

Obsessions are usually accompanied by what are known as compulsive behaviours – actions that patients feel compelled to take in order to counteract the anxiety caused by their fears. So, for example, a patient with an obsession about hygiene may wash their hands repeatedly during the day.

Surprising as it may seem, the best way to deal with obsessions is not to ignore them, but to acknowledge them. Why? For one thing, it is well known that the more you try not to think about something, the more you will think about it. For another, learning to accept the obsession makes it easier for the patient to devise ways to keep them under control. For all this to be effective, though, the person must do their best to resist their compulsions. As with mood swings, exercise and relaxation can considerably lessen the anxiety caused by obsession.

'Surprising as it may seem, the best way to deal with obsessions is not to ignore them, but to acknowledge them.'

Overactivity

Overactivity is a characteristic symptom of attention deficit hyperactivity disorder (ADHD). It includes many different types of behaviours, like fidgeting, inability to stay seated for long periods of time, excessive wandering or pacing, and general restlessness.

You will find that exercise can be very effective at reducing overactivity. This is because it helps the overactive person run off excessive energy and, if performed before focused activities, exercise can also help improve the person's concentration and attention. The type of exercise varies depending on the patient's age. In general, walks, gardening and dancing are popular for an adult with ADHD.

Short bouts of exercise during the day may be better than concentrating all the physical activity in one slot.

Aggressive behaviours

Many patients with a dementia illness, especially Alzheimer's, develop a range of aggressive behaviours at some point during the course of the disease. These can be verbal, such as yelling, swearing and screaming, or physical, like hitting, punching or kicking.

Interventions that have been reported to be effective at reducing aggression in patients with dementia or other mental disorders include:

- Avoiding stressful environments, such as places with too many people and excessive noise.

- Establishing a routine, whereby the person can do the same things every day at the same time and in the same way. Once you have established a routine, do your best not to disrupt it.

- Providing regular opportunities for calming activities, such as listening to music, aromatherapy, massage and exercise (see also chapter 9 for more activity ideas).

- Maintaining a balance between time spent doing activities and rest time.

Careful observation is also very important. If you spot the early signs of an episode of agitation, you may be able to take action before it turns into aggression.

So what should you look for? In most cases, changes in tone of voice, facial expressions and gestures are the first clues that something is wrong.

- Do they raise their voice?

- Do they avoid looking at you while you are talking to them?

- Do their eyes move quickly from side to side?

- Do they appear increasingly restless?

- Do they tremble or start pacing?

- Do they suddenly become too quiet?

'If your loved one's behaviour doesn't seem to improve, try distracting them. The idea is to be able to redirect their attention to things that take their mind off what is causing their agitation, before they become aggressive.'

Any of the above may indicate that your loved one is about to become aggressive. Make sure that all their basic needs are met, and that they are not in pain, thirsty, hungry, tired or need to go to the bathroom. If their behaviour doesn't seem to improve, try distracting them. The idea is to be able to redirect their attention to things that take their mind off what is causing their agitation, before they become aggressive. This means one thing: you have to act quickly. Experts recommend the following strategies:

- Offering the person a favourite object to hold, or a snack.

- Asking for help. For example, you may want to say something like: 'I need to water the plants in the garden and I'd love to have your help.'

- Taking a walk together.

- Looking at a photo album or the view from a window.

Tip

Find out what objects work best at distracting your loved one during a crisis, and keep them at hand in several boxes around the house. Place some items in a small bag and carry it with you when going out with your loved one.

If you are with other people and nothing seems to work, gently take your loved one by the arm and lead them to a quiet corner or another room while reassuring them.

What if the person becomes aggressive anyway?

In this case, you must ensure you approach them in a way that doesn't add to their feelings of anger. A great deal of research has been conducted on this topic. The results consistently show that the chances of successfully dealing with episodes of aggression in people with a mental illness are greater if carers follow these steps:

- Remain calm and try to reassure your loved one – talk with them gently, while smiling and keeping eye contact.

- Avoid confrontation – continue to communicate love and affection. Say something that shows you understand your loved one's feelings of anger and frustration.

- Provide reassurance in any way you can – you may want to hug your loved one or hold their hand. Make sure you ask their permission to do so first. If your attempts result in them hitting your hand away, just stand back and keep talking with a friendly and soothing tone of voice, until they calm down.

- Don't panic – it is crucial that you reassure them that you are in control of the situation and know how to handle it.

- Be aware of your body language when trying to calm your loved one down – avoid expressions and gestures that may unintentionally show anger, such as frowning or putting your hands on your hips.

- Remember that distractions can help, especially if you need to keep your loved one away from objects that could cause harm to themselves, you or other people.

- Keep at a safe distance, in case they attempt to strike.

Hallucinations and delusions

People who experience hallucinations see, hear, touch, smell or taste something that is not really there. For instance, they may see a stranger in the house or hear the voice of a person that is not present. Delusions are false beliefs, like thinking that someone is stealing or that a dead relative is alive. Ideally, you should be able to stop hallucinations and delusions before they happen. Usually, both are preceded by increasing anxiety and restless behaviour, like constantly pacing up and down or saying the same thing over and over again. The same distraction techniques described in the previous section to help patients with aggressive behaviour can help prevent hallucinations and delusions.

However, should your loved one have a delusion or hallucination, here is an example to show how you should deal with it.

Let's assume your loved one – who retired from their job a long time ago – wakes you in the middle of the night saying they need to get ready to go to work. Don't tell them that this is not possible because they don't have a job anymore. But don't tell a lie and pretend that you will help them get ready.

What you should do is try to understand what your loved one is attempting to tell you with their behaviour; that is, you should try to understand the feelings behind the delusion. In this case, the person is probably missing their job and their life before the mental illness, when they had a role in the community. So, the best way to help them is by sharing their feelings and allowing them to talk about their emotions. For example, you may want to say something like, 'You really loved your job. Tell me something about it.'

This approach is called 'validation', and was originally developed in the US by Nomi Feil. 'If we manage our disoriented loved ones with lies or confrontation, they don't feel understood', says European expert in validation, Dr Cinzia Siviero, from the Castellini Foundation in Milan. 'On the other hand, if we use the validation approach, the person will feel welcomed. Not only that. They will gradually put their trust in us and will develop an increased sense of self-confidence.'

Case study

'Yesterday, mum said to me she was ready to drive to pick up my dad from the hospital. I didn't say that dad passed away a long time ago. I didn't tell her that she doesn't drive anymore because she has Alzheimer's either. Instead, I showed her a picture of her wedding day. She is pretty and dad looks so happy. Mum started talking about her wedding day, and of how she met dad. She eventually forgot that she "needed" to go the hospital to pick up dad, and we had one of our best trips down memory lane.'

Ruth, aged 58.

Summing Up

As a carer of someone with a mental illness, one of your main priorities is to help the person in your care overcome cognitive and language difficulties that may affect their ability to interact with others. You need to implement strategies that enable them to perform everyday activities as successfully and independently as possible. In addition, you must become familiar with effective ways for dealing with the most common behavioural problems, such as obsessions, mood swings, aggression, hallucinations and delusions.

Here is a quick checklist of the main recommendations:

- Avoid doing or saying things that could make your loved one feel embarrassed or ashamed of their illness.

- Make sure they know they are loved and still important.

- Some mental illnesses become worse over time. Make sure you adopt helpful strategies as the disease progresses.

- Simplify task, so as to ensure their successful completion. Break them down into several simple steps, provide plenty of verbal prompts and give a practical demonstration if necessary.

- Pay careful attention to behaviour that may indicate unmet needs, such as hunger, thirst and so on, and address them immediately.

For more information see *Alzheimer's – The Essential Guide* (Need2Know).

Chapter Nine

Caring for the Elderly

The older population in the Western world is expanding at a staggering rate. In the UK, the number of people aged 50 and over has increased from 13.8 million in 1951 to 20 million in 2003. This corresponds to a staggering 45% increase in just five decades – a figure that is expected to increase by a further 37% by 2031.

One of the consequences of this is that many families have at least one elderly relative living with them who need their care and assistance. This chapter looks at some of the most important aspects of caring for an older person at home.

Understanding ageing

Older adults experience a number of changes that are a normal part of the ageing process. Wrinkles and white hair are the most noticeable of these changes, together with a general decline in physical functions, like hearing, vision and mobility. In addition, the internal organs (heart, lungs and liver) become weaker, and so does the immune system.

Not a disease

Although such changes make an elderly person more vulnerable to illness, it is important to remember that getting older is not a disease. Ageing is a normal process we all go through. Some older adults get ill and others don't, just like younger people. Despite common belief, old age is not the worst time of life, a survey conducted in the United States in 2000 found that for almost half of a sample of individuals aged 65 and beyond, old age was the best time of life (Braun and Cheang, 2002).

'Ageing is a normal process we all go through. Some older adults get ill and others don't, just like younger people.'

Preventing falls

Falls occur annually for around 30% of individuals older than 65 years of age, many of whom experience serious injuries which can lead to permanent disability or death. Fall prevention is, therefore, one of the most important aspects of caring for an elderly person. This section gives you information and practical advice on how to reduce your loved one's risk of falling and cope with falls when these occur, according to the latest research.

'Encourage physical activity, such as walking, cycling and tai chi, as well as heel raises, sit-to-stand, reaching and seated exercises (e.g. knee flexions and extensions).'

What you can do

The table on page 89 lists the most common causes of falls in the elderly and how to address them.

Preventing fractures

Nearly 80% of fall-related deaths are the consequence of injuries to the head, hips and legs. Hip fractures are a particularly serious problem. It is estimated that 25% of elderly people with a hip fracture die within 12 months. If your loved one is aged 85 years or older, their risk of having a fall-related hip fracture is 15 times greater than in those aged 60 to 65.

The good news is that there are strategies that can help you deal with this problem. For example, you can reduce your loved one's risk of fractures by encouraging them to wear hip protectors. These come in a variety of designs and sizes to suit every taste and ensure comfortable fit. They are not bulky and can easily be worn over, or under, clothing. Although the evidence is somewhat inconsistent, an increasing number of studies show that, if used regularly, hip protectors can reduce considerably the likelihood of fall-related hip fractures.

Experts also recommend calcium and vitamin D supplements. However, the evidence about their effectiveness is inconclusive. This is true for both vitamin D alone and combinations of vitamin D and calcium, although there are examples of successful outcomes associated with such interventions. These include a study by researchers at the University of Zurich in Switzerland showing that daily administration of vitamin D for three to five months can reduce the risk of falling by 19% (Bischoff-Ferrari et al., 2009).

Causes	Interventions
Environmental hazards	Eliminate clutter, rugs, loose carpets, as well as electrical and telephone cords. Keep the floor dry. Clean up spills immediately. Place non-slip mats in the bathroom – including rubber shower/bath mats – and in the kitchen. Install handrails in hallways, bathrooms and stairs. Check that the height of the bed is such that when the person sits on it their feet are flat on the floor.
Eyesight and hearing problems	Ensure regular hearing and eyesight tests are done. Make sure your loved one wears their glasses and/or hearing aids. Check that the former are clean and unscratched and that the latter are in good working order. All rooms should be well illuminated; the stairs should have a light switch at the top and the bottom. Apply coloured tape at the edge of steps to make them more visible.
Poor balance	Encourage physical activity, such as walking, cycling and tai chi, as well as heel raises, sit-to-stand, reaching and seated exercises (e.g. knee flexions and extensions).
Sudden drop in blood pressure	Remind them to get up slowly from sitting or lying positions, especially after eating.
Medication	Ask the GP to regularly review dosage and administration frequency of laxatives, diuretics, antidepressants and sedatives.
Insomnia and incontinence	Remind your loved one to turn the light on when getting out of bed at night, and to avoid running to reach the bathroom. Ensure there is a light switch or a lamp near the bed.
Foot problems	Regularly check your loved one's feet for problems that may impair walking ability, like bunions, calluses, injuries and poor blood circulation (when feet are persistently cold).
At-risk behaviours	Encourage your loved one not to: ▪ Wear clothes that drag on the floor, slippers, high-heeled shoes and socks, including non-slip socks. ▪ Carry things up and down the stairs. ▪ Step on stools or chairs to reach high cabinets or cupboards. ▪ Climb stairs without holding on to handrails. ▪ Run to the telephone or front door.
Using a walking rollator	Make sure your loved one knows how to use their walking rollator correctly – and safely. For instance, they should know how to lock and unlock the brakes and should never attempt to sit in an unlocked rollator.

What if your loved one falls?

Tip

If your loved one has a fall, don't give them food, drinks or medication while waiting for the ambulance. Instead, talk to them. They are likely to be scared and confused, and need you to reassure them that everything will be all right.

If your loved one has a fall and is lying on the floor, you shouldn't move them or try to pick them up, especially if they are unconscious or in pain. Cover them up with a blanket to keep them warm and call the emergency services right away.

'If your loved one falls and then gets up from the floor with little or no help, they should still seek medical help.'

If your loved one falls and then gets up from the floor with little or no help, they should still seek medical help. Even though the fall may seem nothing serious, an examination by their GP will help prevent missing important, but not obvious, injuries needing treatment.

How to deal with incontinence

Tip

Encourage your loved one to perform pelvic floor exercises. These involve exercising the muscles that support the bladder, helping to improve its control. You can find these exercises on the Bladder and Bowel Foundation website (see help list).

Incontinence is another common problem in older adults. In the UK, it affects approximately six million individuals, the majority of whom are over the age of 65.

If your elderly loved one has urinary or bowel incontinence, or both, here are some ways you can help:

- Ensure regular visits to the bathroom, e.g. every two hours, and always after meals. This will reduce the risk of accidents and the need for nappies, in turn helping your loved one maintain their self-confidence.

- If they need a cane to move around, make sure this is always within their reach so they can get to the bathroom in time. Also, make sure their clothes are easy to undo.

- Coffee and alcohol consumption should be kept to a minimum because it increases urination. Similarly, foods rich in fibre, like bread, beans, cereals and potatoes, as well as exercising after getting up from bed in the morning, increase bowel movements, thus making bowel incontinence worse.

- If your loved one spends time outdoors, check in advance that, wherever they go, there are bathroom facilities, and that these are easily accessible.

More incontinence tips are available from the Bladder and Bowel Foundation (see help list).

Tip

Keep a written record of:

- Where and when incontinence accidents happen.

- What your loved one eats and drinks.

- Colour and consistency of stools.

It will be easier for your GP to determine the cause of the incontinence and identify most effective treatments if you note down the above.

Tell the GP

Always tell the GP about incontinence problems in your loved one. Both urinary and bowel incontinence can be signs of much more serious medical conditions, such as congestive heart failure, and therefore need to be promptly addressed.

If an accident happens

Older people are particularly vulnerable to feelings of embarrassment after an incontinence episode, so the first thing you should do is to provide reassurance. Don't say anything that can make your loved one feel guilty, embarrassed or ashamed. Smile, make a joke and use humour to lighten up the situation.

- Gently clean them with soap and warm water – don't use toilet paper, as it can irritate the skin.

- Pat dry.

- Apply a zinc oxide-based barrier cream.

It is important to ensure that they drink the recommended daily amount of water, which is about eight glasses, according to the Food Standards Agency. Reducing their fluid intake does not improve incontinence and is dangerous, as it can lead to dehydration.

Dehydration can be fatal

Our body needs to be hydrated in order to function well and that is why we become thirsty if there is too little water in our body. If we don't drink, we develop dehydration, which can lead to infections, mental confusion, coma and death.

The problem with age is that the sense of thirst diminishes. As a result, the elderly are at increased risk of dehydration and often require hospital care if they develop this condition.

Know how to prevent it

Here is a checklist of things you can do to prevent dehydration in the elderly, as reported by researchers at City University, London, in the journal *Nursing Older People*:

- Remind your loved one to drink regularly.

- Offer them water and fruit juice several times during the day.

'The problem with age is that the sense of thirst diminishes. As a result, the elderly are at increased risk of dehydration and often require hospital care if they develop this condition.'

- Keep drinks fresh and clearly visible.

- Address any impairment that may affect their ability to drink. For example, give them straws if they can't open their mouth, use thickeners if they have swallowing problems, and open bottles and cartons if they are too frail to do it by themselves.

Also, be alert for the signs and symptoms of dehydration, such as:

- Headache.

- Dizziness.

- Tiredness.

- Dry mouth.

- Dark-coloured urine.

Any of these may indicate that dehydration is setting in and that treatment is required to prevent complications. If you notice them, call the GP.

(Source: Holman et al., 2005.)

Insomnia

Difficulty sleeping is a common, but underestimated, problem in the elderly. There is a general misconception that it is an inevitable consequence of getting older, whereas it is in fact a condition with potentially serious, and even fatal, complications.

Diabetes, hypertension and memory loss are just a few of the problems your elderly loved one may develop if they don't sleep enough. Furthermore, their mortality risk can increase. Findings in the journal *Sleep* show that a lack of sleep almost doubles the likelihood of dying from all causes (Ferrie et al., 2007).

Prevention

So, what can you do to prevent insomnia in your loved one? Here are the top six recommendations by sleep experts:

'Difficulty sleeping is a common, but underestimated, problem in the elderly. There is a general misconception that it is an inevitable consequence of getting older, whereas it is in fact a condition with potentially serious, and even fatal, complications.'

- Encourage your elderly loved one not to consume too much coffee and other caffeine-rich drinks, like cola and tea, especially before going to sleep. And remember, chocolate and cocoa are also rich in caffeine.

- Discourage daytime naps. If they can't be avoided, make sure they last no longer than half an hour and are taken before 3pm.

- Encourage exercise. Think of activities your loved one might like; for example, many elderly people enjoy walking and gardening. Not a lot of exercise is needed – 30 minutes on most weekdays will be enough.

- At night, avoid disturbing your loved one's sleep with noise. Close their bedroom door and keep the volume of the TV/radio down.

Treatment

If problems with sleep develop, your GP may or may not recommend medication. Until recently, the accepted view has been that insomnia is best treated with drugs. But an increasing number of studies show that these have harmful side effects and should, therefore, be considered only as the last resort.

Following are some non-drug approaches that may help:

- If your loved one doesn't fall asleep within about 20 minutes of going to bed, they should get up, go into another room and not return to bed until they feel sleepy again.

- It is also crucial that they get up every morning at the same time, regardless of how much they managed to sleep during the night.

- They should use their bedroom only for sleeping, not for watching TV, listening to the radio or reading.

- They should spend some time every day engaging in relaxing activities, like taking a scented bath, massage, listening to favourite music, reading or going out with friends.

Depression

Recent estimates indicate that about 11% of men and 17% of women over 65 years of age suffer from some form of depression. So if you are caring for an elderly person, the chances are that you may have to deal with this condition at some point.

The interventions described in chapter 6 can also help address this problem in older people, and reduce the risk of depression if they are not affected by the condition. In essence, you need to ensure that your loved one has an extended social network of family and friends, keeps physically and mentally active, and enjoys doing activities. According to recent research, another effective way to protect older people from depression is to help them continue to practise their faith or spiritual belief. In 2009, Law and Sbarra published a study in the *Journal of Aging and Health* showing that elderly people who regularly go to church are less likely to develop symptoms of depression.

Activities: the key to successful ageing

> **Tip**
>
> Whatever activity you may be considering for your loved one, make sure it is something they truly like and can do.

'Several studies suggest that religious activities, like other activities, play an important role in successfully coping with the many changes that come with age.'

Several studies suggest that religious activities, like other activities, play an important role in successfully coping with the many changes that come with age, like loss of functioning and independence, and which may undermine the wellbeing of an elderly person.

According to a team of scientists at the University of San Francisco, individuals as old as 92 with high levels of engagement in activities feel better, physically and mentally, than elders who don't engage in activities. Not only that, they also show greater adaptability to negative life situations, like illness and death of a loved one (Van Leuven, 2009). Other research has looked into the specific therapeutic effects that different types of activities can have on older people. The table overleaf shows the main findings.

Activity	Therapeutic effects
Cognitive games (e.g. cards, dominoes, puzzles, Scrabble, Bingo, etc.)	Helps maintain and improve memory and reasoning skills.
Reminiscence (e.g. looking through old photos and talking about the past)	Stimulates memory and improves self-esteem.
Painting, drawing, clay modelling and writing	Promotes sense of achievement; helps maintain and improve hand-eye co-ordination and fine motor skills.
Playing and listening to music, singing	Facilitates relaxation; reduces risk of depression by evoking positive feelings.
Looking after a pet	Provides sense of purpose; reduces blood pressure, heart rate and anxiety.
Going out (to the shops, the cinema and so on) and day trips	Helps maintain an interest in life, thus alleviating feelings of sadness.
Household chores and volunteering activities	Makes one feel useful, important and still involved in family and community life.
Religious/spiritual activities (attending mass, praying, etc.)	Prevents depression; gives sense of purpose; helps preserve cognition.
Exercise (e.g. walking, dancing, gardening, cycling, swimming and tai chi)	Promotes physical and mental health, while reducing fall risk.
Playing with grandchildren and other forms of interaction with younger generations	Enhances sense of self-worth; gives sense of purpose; helps prevent depression.
Computer-based activities (e.g. emailing, searching for information, joining networking groups)	Keeps the elderly mentally and socially active.

Summing Up

Caring for an elderly loved one requires commitment and a desire to treat the person with respect and dignity. You need to be familiar with strategies that help prevent, or cope with, the most common problems associated with ageing – like falls, incontinence, dehydration, insomnia and depression. Also, ensure regular involvement in social and leisure activities for enhanced physical and mental wellbeing.

For more information please see *Insomnia – The Essential Guide* and *Depression – The Essential Guide* (Need2Know).

Chapter Ten

Caring for a Dying Loved One

The terminal stage of a disease, when a person is beyond hope of recovery, is undoubtedly a difficult time. However, this is also a time of great tenderness – an opportunity to fill your loved one's last days of life with loving kindness, while providing the best possible care.

What is palliative care?

Your major goal is to make sure that the person in your care is free from pain, comfortable and feels loved. This is at the heart of what is known as 'palliative care'. It aims to enhance the quality of remaining life to ensure that death occurs with minimum suffering, in dignity and according to the wishes of the dying person.

To find out more about this approach, contact one of the many palliative care teams available in the UK and Ireland. The charity Help the Hospices has a searchable database online (see help list).

Pain relief: not just with medication

Unfortunately, many terminally ill patients experience chronic, sometimes excruciating, pain. This increases their physical and emotional distress, so it needs to be addressed promptly and effectively. The general recommendation is round-the-clock administration of pain-killers, depending on the pain severity, at whatever dose is required to relieve distress.

'Your major goal is to make sure that the person in your care is free from pain, comfortable and feels loved. This is at the heart of what is known as "palliative care".'

Of course, the doctor will give you specific guidance on what pain medication to use, and how and when to use them. However, there are other things you can do to make your loved one feel better. For example, a study conducted by researchers at the University of Colorado shows that massage can significantly reduce pain in patients with late-stage cancer, and its effect is immediate (Kutner et al., 2008). In another study, this time by scientists at Florida Atlantic University, gently caressing the person's hands or forehead while speaking with a soothing voice reduced pain in people with dementia. The scientists also found that allowing patients to listen to their favourite music lowered osteoarthritis-related pain (McCaffrey and Freeman, 2003).

But what if your loved one cannot tell you that they are in pain? This is the case, for example, for people with a dementia illness like Alzheimer's disease. You need to look at their behaviour closely to know if they are suffering. Is the person:

- More agitated than usual?
- Groaning?
- Frowning?
- Clenching their teeth?
- Shaking?
- Constantly holding one part of their body?
- Sweating?

If you have noticed at least one of the above, your loved one is likely to be in pain. You need to tell the doctor and make sure that appropriate treatment is given immediately.

Prevent skin breakdown

The skin of a dying person is usually very fragile. Several factors contribute to this, including limited or no mobility and incontinence. As a result, skin tears, bruising and ulcers are common. These can complicate and add considerably to the person's pain, and should be prevented.

You can use the same techniques for preventing pressure ulcers described in chapter 6. Here is a quick reminder of what to do:

'Gently caressing the person's hands or forehead while speaking with a soothing voice has been found to reduce pain in people with dementia.'

- Thoroughly inspect your loved one's skin twice a day. Look, in particular, for redness, rashes, blisters and cuts.

- Change their position every two hours or less, using turning sheets to reduce friction.

- If they use incontinence nappies, check these often so you can change them as soon as they are wet or dirty.

Should damaged skin areas be already present, keep them clean at all times. Wash them gently with drinking water or saline solution. Don't use antiseptics like hydrogen peroxide, as these can further irritate the person's skin.

Helping with eating

Ensuring effective pain prevention and relief is just one of the challenges you will be dealing with. As your loved one moves towards the end of life, their ability to eat independently deteriorates, partly as a result of chewing and swallowing problems. This puts them at risk of choking and breathing food and liquids into the lungs. Therefore, you need to make sure they eat and drink enough, while keeping the risk of mealtime accidents to a minimum.

Here are some guidelines to help you achieve this:

- At this stage of illness, it's likely you will be spoon-feeding your loved one. Before you start, make certain they are sitting upright and are alert.

- Ensure the room is quiet, with no distractions, noise or people coming and going.

- Sit in front of them so you can see immediately if there is a problem (e.g. coughing, choking or pain).

- Offer half a teaspoon of pureed food at a time and wait for them to swallow completely before offering other food.

- It's also helpful to offer them something to drink every two or three spoonfuls, as this makes it easier to clear the mouth of any food residue.

- Consider that adding thickeners to drinks reduces considerably the risk of choking and breathing liquid into the lungs.

If the person refuses to eat

There will be a point at which your loved one refuses to eat. This is a normal part of the dying process and is associated with the body's release of natural pain relief chemicals called endorphins. Consequently, it is best not to resort to force-feeding because this would affect their ability to fight pain, in turn increasing their suffering. The same goes for artificial feeding, which has been found to increase the risk of ulcers and infections.

'There will be a point at which your loved one refuses to eat. This is a normal part of the dying process and is associated with the body's release of natural pain relief chemicals called endorphins.'

How to recognise when death is near

Key signs of approaching death include the following:

- Mental confusion or unconsciousness.
- Restlessness, also called terminal agitation.
- Involuntary movements.
- Arms and legs become increasingly cold.
- Lips, earlobes and fingers turn blue.
- Irregular breathing.
- Rattling or gurgling, caused by excessive mucus in the mouth and at the back of the throat.
- Total loss of bladder and bowel control.
- Open jaw.
- Fixed eyes with large pupils.

There are some actions that will help your loved one when they are approaching the end of their life:

- Keep them warm with blankets.
- Apply a moist tissue to their face and forehead to provide relief.
- Raise their head with pillows to facilitate breathing.
- Gently remove mucus from the lips with a soft towel.

- Clean them immediately after incontinence occurs.

- Ensure pain relief with medication is continued.

- Keep the room humidified and the lights dimmed.

- Moisten their lips often to prevent cracks. Ice chips and fruit juice also help, if they can still swallow.

- Provide reassurance. Keep talking to your loved one with a calm and soothing voice, even if they seem unaware of what's happening around them.

Be there for them

The last point is of particular importance, as palliative care is mostly about being able to communicate tenderness, affection and love. Even if the person is too weak or unable to talk, they can still hear your voice and perceive your presence. And the benefit that comes from this – as well as from small acts of loving kindness like holding and caressing – is invaluable. Studies show it can make the difference between the person maintaining physical and emotional comfort until the end of life – or not.

Examples of things you can do include:

- Gently hugging your loved one.

- Holding their hands.

- Caressing their hair.

- Listening to calm music together.

- Softly singing their favourite song or tune.

- Telling them a story.

- Reminiscing about happy events of the past.

'Provide reassurance. Keep talking to your loved one with a calm and soothing voice, even if they seem unaware of what's happening around them.'

Coping with loss

Dealing with the grief caused by the death of someone close to you is a long, hard process. However, it is also a necessary step towards coming to terms with the new situation. It will help you accept that your loved one is no longer with you, and will give you the strength and encouragement to move on.

The stages of bereavement

Although different people tend to cope with grief in different ways, most go through the same stages:

- Shock – you don't really believe that your loved one has died. In a way, the sense of disbelief is helpful, because it allows you to go through the many practical issues you need to address at this stage, like organising a funeral service. Information about what you need to do first when someone dies is available from the Bereavement Advice Centre (see help list).

- Sadness – as you gradually become aware of the fact that your loved one has passed away, you may feel extremely low. You may lose interest in activities you used to enjoy. It is normal at this stage to experience feelings of anger or guilt.

- Acceptance – you eventually come to terms with your loss. The sadness begins to lessen, and you learn to live with and adapt to the new situation.

For more information and advice on coping with bereavement, see *Bereavement – The Essential Guide* (Need2Know).

How you can help yourself

Failure to deal with your emotions will put you at risk of depression and other serious health problems. Here is a quick checklist of things you should do to help yourself. Tick 'yes' for the ones you are doing already and 'no' for those you are not. This will give you a clearer idea of the areas you still need to address to gently work your way towards recovery.

Yes No

☐ ☐ Share your feelings with a friend or a professional counsellor. You can find a list of qualified therapists on the British Association for Counselling and Psychotherapy's website (see help list).

☐ ☐ Join a support group. Cruse Bereavement Care (see help list), for example, is one of the largest in the UK.

☐ ☐ Get enough sleep, eat healthy and exercise. Stay away from alcohol and cigarettes.

☐ ☐ Dedicate time to your favourite activities. For example, go to the cinema or have a day out with your best friend.

☐ ☐ Reward yourself for your progress, however small. Buy yourself a little present or treat every now and then.

☐ ☐ Reminisce about your loved one and the good things they brought into your life.

☐ ☐ Consider bereavement services and setting up memorials. Many grieving people find this of great comfort. You can find a directory on the Bereavement Services Directory's website. The online memorial charity Much Loved gives bereaved people the opportunity to publish tributes for their loved ones online (see help list).

Summing Up

When caring for a dying loved one, it is important to attend to both their physical and emotional needs. This will ensure that their last days are comfortable, free from pain and filled with tenderness and love.

- Make certain that they receive their pain-relieving medication around the clock.

- Help enhance the medication's effect with music, massage or by gently caressing hands or forehead.

- If your loved one can't talk, be alert for behaviours that may indicate that they are in pain, such as increased agitation, groaning or shaking.

- Prevent skin breakdown by inspecting their body often during the day and changing their position at least every two hours. Keep clean any area of skin damage that might be present with gentle washing.

- Assist with eating to reduce the risk of choking and aspiration of food and liquids into the lungs. But don't force your loved one if they refuse to eat.

- When death is near, make sure pain relief with medication is continued, provide comfort and let your loved one know that you are there for them – talk, reassure and hug.

- After your loved one's death, deal with your emotions – share your feelings with someone and take good care of yourself. This will reduce your risk of major health problems, like depression, and will shorten your way towards recovery.

Help List

Benefit Enquiry Line (UK)

Red Rose House, Lancaster Road, Preston, Lancashire, PR1 1HB
Tel: 0800 882 200 (helpline: Monday to Friday, 8.30am-6.30pm,
Saturday, 9am-1pm)
BEL-Customer-Services@dwp.gsi.gov.uk
www.direct.gov.uk/disability-money
Provides general advice and information for disabled people and carers on the
range of benefits available.

Bereavement Advice Centre

Ryon Hill, Ryon Hill Park, Warwick Road, Stratford upon Avon, CV37 0UX
Tel: 0800 634 9494 (helpline)
www.bereavementadvice.org
This is a non-profit organisation which provides free advice on the practical
aspects of what to do when someone dies.

Bereavement Services Directory

www.bereavement-services.org
Here you may look up the contact details of over 1,000 burial authorities and
private company operators, 250 crematoria and nearly 200 natural burial
ground operators, representing more than 3,500 individual sites for burial and
cremation.

Bladder and Bowel Foundation

SATRA Innovation Park, Rockingham Road, Kettering, Northants, NN16 9JH
Tel: 0845 345 0165
info@bladderandbowelfoundation.org
www.bladderandbowelfoundation.org
The UK's largest, non-profit making, advocacy charity providing help,
information and support for all types of bladder and bowel related problems,
for patients, carers and healthcare professionals.

Blue Badge Scheme

www.direct.gov.uk
A scheme that allows holders of a blue badge to park for free in designated spaces. Click 'disabled people' then 'blue badge scheme' to find the relevant section of the website.

British Association for Counselling and Psychotherapy

www.bacp.co.uk
A professional registering body for counsellors. Has a find-a-therapist section. You can also call their client information line for help finding a suitable counsellor.

British-Sign

Honeysuckle Cottage, Les Dunes, Vazon, Castel, Guernsey, GY5 7LQ
Tel: 02071 173829
info@british-sign.co.uk
www.british-sign.co.uk
Commercial organisation providing online British Sign Language courses.

Carers Direct

Tel: 0808 802 0202 (helpline)
www.nhs.uk/CarersDirect
Carers support and information online. Find advice on respite breaks, Carer's Allowance and assessments.

Carers UK

20 Great Dover Street, London, SE1 4LX
Tel: 020 7378 4999
info@carersuk.org
www.carersuk.org
A membership organisation of carers, led by carers for carers.

Childline

Tel: 0800 1111 (helpline)
www.childline.org.uk

Offers a free 24-hour helpline for children in distress or danger. Trained volunteer counsellors comfort, advise and protect children and young people who may feel they have nowhere else to turn.

Citizens Advice Bureau (CAB)

www.citizensadvice.org.uk
With branches all over the country, the CAB offers free advice on finance and legal matters. Visit the website to locate your local branch.

Cruse Bereavement Care

PO Box 800, Richmond, Surrey, TW9 1UR
Tel: 0844 477 9400 (helpline)
helpline@cruse.org.uk
www.crusebereavementcare.org.uk
Cruse is a national charity which offers independent advice and support to adults and children. There are branches all over the country, many of which offer one-to-one counselling, a telephone helpline and support groups.

Directgov

www.direct.gov.uk
The UK government's digital service for people in England and Wales, with information and practical advice about public services.

Disabled Living Foundation (DLF)

380-4 Harrow Road, London, W9 2HU
Tel: 020 7289 6111
info@dlf.org.uk
helpline@dlf.org.uk
www.dlf.org.uk
Provides information on disability equipment, day-to-day household gadgets, new technologies and training techniques.

Disabled Persons Railcard

Rail Travel Made Easy, PO Box 11631, Laurencekirk, AB30 9AA
Tel: 0845 605 0525
disability@atoc.org

www.disabledpersons-railcard.co.uk
If you have a disability which makes travelling difficult, you get a third off most rail fares in the UK.

Guide Dogs for the Blind Association

Burghfield Common, Reading, RG7 3YG
Tel: 0118 983 5555
guidedogs@guidedogs.org.uk
www.guidedogs.org.uk
Provides mobility and freedom to blind and partially sighted people. Guide Dogs for the Blind Association also campaign for the rights of people with visual impairment, educate the public about eye care and fund eye disease research.

Hearing Dogs for Deaf People

The Grange, Wycombe Road, Saunderton, Princes Risborough, Buckinghamshire, HP27 9NS
Tel: 01844 348 100
info@hearingdogs.org.uk
www.hearingdogs.org.uk
National organisation which works to help deaf and hard of hearing people through the training and placement of specially trained dogs.

Help the Hospices

Hospice House, 34-44 Britannia Street, London, WC1X 9JG
Tel: 020 7520 8200
info@helpthehospices.org.uk
www.helpthehospices.org.uk
The leading charity supporting hospice care throughout the UK.

Macular Disease Society

PO Box 1870, Andover, SP10 9AD
Tel: 01264 350551
info@maculardisease.org
www.maculardisease.org

Charity aiming to build confidence and independence for those with central vision impairment. The only UK charity dedicated to helping people with macular degeneration.

Motability

Motability Operations, City Gate House, 22 Southwark Bridge Road, London E1 9HB
Tel: 0845 456 4566
www.motability.co.uk
A national UK charity which helps disabled people and their families to become more mobile.

Much Loved

www.muchloved.com
A charity where bereaved parties can create an online tribute to their loved one.

National Institute for Clinical Excellence (NICE)

MidCity Place, 71 High Holborn, London, WC1V 6NA
Tel: 0845 003 7780
nice@nice.org.uk
www.nice.org.uk
Independent organisation responsible for providing national guidance on the promotion of good health and the prevention and treatment of ill health.

The Princess Royal Trust for Carers

Unit 14, Bourne Court, Southend Road, Woodford Green, Essex, IG8 8HD
Tel: 0844 800 4361
info@carers.org
www.carers.org
The largest provider of comprehensive carers' support services in the UK. Through its unique network of 144 independently managed Carers' Centres, it currently provides quality information, advice and support services to over 400,000 carers.

Ramblers Association

2nd Floor Camelford House, 87-90 Albert Embankment, London, SE1 7TW
Tel: 020 7339 8500
ramblers@ramblers.org.uk
www.ramblers.org.uk
Campaigns to protect and improved access to the countryside and operates a network of local groups that organise walks and events.

RNIB

105 Judd Street, London, WC1H 9NE
Tel: 0303 123 9999 (helpline)
helpline@rnib.org.uk
www.rnib.org.uk
Supports blind and partially sighted people. Their priorities are to stop people from losing their sight unnecessarily, to support independent living for people with sight loss or blindness, and to creative an inclusive society.

RNID

19-23 Featherstone Street, London, EC1Y 8SL
Tel: 0808 808 0123 (information line)
informationline@rnid.org.uk
www.rnid.org.uk
RNID is the charity working to create a world where deafness or hearing loss do not limit or determine opportunity, and where people value their hearing. It works by campaigning and lobbying, raising awareness of deafness and hearing loss, promoting hearing health, providing services and through social, medical and technical research.

Samaritans

Chris, PO Box 9090, Stirling, FK8 2SA
Tel: 084 57 909090 (helpline)
1850 609090 (helpline Ireland)
jo@samaritans.org
www.samaritans.org

Samaritans provides a confidential support service for people who are depressed, feeling distressed or considering suicide. The service is available 24 hours a day in the UK and Ireland.

Shopmobility

PO Box 6641, Christchurch, BH23 9DQ
Tel: 08456 442 446
info@shopmobilityuk.org
www.shopmobilityuk.org
A federation of more than 250 schemes providing scooters and wheelchairs for shoppers with mobility problems.

Young Carers Project (YCP)

The Princess Royal Trust for Carers, Unit 14, Bourne Court, Southern Road, Woodford Green, Essex, IG8 8HD
Tel: 0844 800 4361
info@carers.org
help@carers.org
www.youngcarers.net
The largest provider of comprehensive carers' support services in the UK. Through its unique network of 85 young carers services, it currently provides quality information, advice and support services to approximately 25,000 young carers.

References

Ahola, K, *et al.*, 'Burnout as a predictor of all-cause mortality among industrial employees: a 10-year prospective register-linkage study', *Journal of Psychosomatic Research*, 2010, vol. 69, pages 51-7.

Barton, J and Pretty, J, 'What is the best dose of nature and green exercise for improving mental health? A multi-study analysis', *Environmental Science and Technology*, 2010, vol. 44, pages 3947-55.

Berman, K and Brodaty, H, 'Psychosocial effects of age-related macular degeneration', *International Psychogeriatrics*, 2006, vol. 18, pages 415-28.

Bischoff-Ferrari, HA, *et al.*, 'Fall prevention with supplemental and active forms of vitamin D: a meta-analysis of randomized controlled trials', *British Medical Journal*, 2009, doi:10.1136/bmj.b3692.

Braun, KL, Cheang, M, *Paraprofessional in Aging: a guidebook for those who care for older adults*, University of Hawai'i, Center on Aging, 2002.

Brooker, D, *Person-centred Dementia Care*, Jessica Kingsley Publishers, London, 2007.

Cohen-Mansfield, J and Werner, P, 'Environmental influences on agitation: an integrative summary of an observational study', *American Journal of Alzheimer's Disease and Other Dementias*, 1995, vol. 10, pages 32-9.

Dewing, J, 'Caring for people with dementia: noise and light', *Nursing Older People*, 2009, vol. 21, pages 34-8.

Duffy, B, *et al.*, 'Burnout among care staff for older adults with dementia', *Dementia*, 2009, vol. 8, pages 515-41.

Feil, N *et al.*, *The Validation Breakthrough: Simple Techniques for Communicating with People with Alzheimer's Type Dementia, second edition*, Health Professions Press, USA, 2002.

Ferrie, JE, *et al.*, 'A prospective study of change in sleep duration: associations with mortality in the Whitehall II cohort', *Sleep*, 2007, vol. 30, pages 1659-66.

Flood, M and Buckwalter, KC, 'Recommendations for mental health care of older adults – part one, an overview of depression and anxiety', *Journal of Gerontological Nursing*, 2009, vol. 35, pages 26-34.

Geda, YE and Rummans,TA, 'Pain: cause of agitation in elderly individuals with dementia', *American Journal of Psychiatry*, 1999, vol. 156, pages 1662-3.

Hellen, CR, *Alzheimer's Disease Activity-focused Care, second edition*, Butterworth Heinemann, Oxford, 1998.

Holman, C, *et al.*, 'Promoting adequate hydration in older people', *Nursing Older People*, 2005, vol. 17, pages 31-2.

Kitaoka, K, *et al.*, 'Burnout and risk factors for arteriosclerotic disease: follow-up study', *Journal of Occupational Health*, 2009, vol. 51, pages 123-31.

Kroger, J and Adair, V, 'Symbolic meanings of valued personal objects in identity transitions in late adulthood', *Identity*, 2008, vol. 8, pages 5-25.

Kutner, JS, *et al.*, 'Massage therapy versus simple touch to improve pain and mood in patients with advanced cancer: a randomized trial', *Annals of Internal Medicines*, 2008, vol. 149, pages 369-79.

Law, R and Sbarra, DA, 'The effects of church attendance and marital status on the longitudinal trajectories of depressed mood among older adults', *Journal of Aging and Health*, 2009, vol. 21, pages 803-23.

Lloyd, M, 'The prevention and management of skin tears', *British Journal of Healthcare Assistant*, 2008, vol. 2, pages 54-7.

McCaffrey, R and Freeman, E, 'Effect of music on chronic osteoarthritis pain in older people', *Journal of Advanced Nursing*, 2003, vol. 44, pages 517-24.

Melamed, S, *et al.*, 'Burnout and risk of type 2 diabetes: a prospective study of apparently healthy employed persons', *Psychosomatic Medicine*, 2006, vol. 68, pages 863-9.

Namazi, KH and Johnson, BD, 'Issues related to behavior and the physical environment: bathing cognitively impaired patients', *Geriatric Nursing*, 1996, vol. 17, pages 238-9.

National Health Service (NHS), *Registered blind and partially sighted people year ending 31 March 2008*, NHS, London, 2008.

National Health Service (NHS), *The prevention and management of pressure ulcers: An educational workbook*, NHS, London, 2009.

National Institute for Clinical Excellence (NICE), *Pressure Ulcer Management: NICE guideline*, NICE, London, 2005.

Office of National Statistics, *Carers*, 2003, www.statistics.gov.uk/CCI/nugget.asp?ID=347&Pos=&ColRank=1&Rank=358, accessed 23 July 2010.

Osse, BH, *et al.*, 'Problems experienced by the informal caregivers of cancer patients and their needs for support', *Cancer Nursing*, 2006, vol. 29, pages 378-88.

Rassin, M, *et al.*, 'Caregivers' role in breaking bad news: patients, doctors, and nurses' points of view', *Cancer Nursing*, 2006, vol. 29, pages 302-8.

Savundranayagam, MY, *et al.*, 'Investigating the effects of communication problems on caregiver burden', *Journal of Gerontology: Social Sciences,* 2005, vol. 60B, pages S48-S55.

Siviero, C *et al.*, 'Vascular dementia: a clinical case managed with the contribution of the validation method', *54th National Congress of the Italian Society of Gerontology and Geriatrics*, December 2-5, 2009, Florence, Italy.

Sloane, PD, *et al.*, 'Effects of person-centered showering and towel bath on bathing-associated aggression, agitation and discomfort in nursing home residents with dementia: A randomized-controlled trial', *Journal of the American Geriatrics Society*, 2004, vol. 52, pages 1795-1804.

Stokes, G, *Challenging Behavior in Dementia: A Person-centered Approach*, Speechmark, Milton Keynes, 2000.

Tan, T and Schneider, MA, 'Humor as a coping strategy for adult-child caregivers of individuals with Alzheimer's Disease', *Geriatric Nursing*, 2009, vol. 30, issue 6, pages 397-408.

Van Leuven, KA, 'Health practices of older adults in good health. Engagement is key', *Journal of Gerontological Nursing*, 2009, doi:10.3928/00989134-20091110-99.

Vance, DE, *et al.*, 'Predictors of agitation in nursing home residents', *Journal of Gerontology: Psychological Sciences*, 2003, vol. 58B, pages 129-37.

Watkinson, S, 'Management of older people with dry and wet age-related macular degeneration', *Nursing Older People*, 2010, vol. 22, pages 21-6.

Wingfield, A, *et al.*, 'Hearing loss in older adulthood. What it is and how it interacts with cognitive performance', *Current Directions in Psychological Science*, 2005, vol. 14, pages 144-8.

Yamada, R and Yamada, K, 'Environmental arrangement for enhancing self-feeding in the elderly with dementia', *Geriatric Nursing*, 2004, vol. 25, pages 52-3.

Need2Know

Need -2- Know

Need - 2 - Know

Available Titles Include ...

Allergies A Parent's Guide
ISBN 978-1-86144-064-8 £8.99

Autism A Parent's Guide
ISBN 978-1-86144-069-3 £8.99

Drugs A Parent's Guide
ISBN 978-1-86144-043-3 £8.99

Dyslexia and Other Learning Difficulties
A Parent's Guide ISBN 978-1-86144-042-6 £8.99

Bullying A Parent's Guide
ISBN 978-1-86144-044-0 £8.99

Epilepsy The Essential Guide
ISBN 978-1-86144-063-1 £8.99

Teenage Pregnancy The Essential Guide
ISBN 978-1-86144-046-4 £8.99

Gap Years The Essential Guide
ISBN 978-1-86144-079-2 £8.99

How to Pass Exams A Parent's Guide
ISBN 978-1-86144-047-1 £8.99

Child Obesity A Parent's Guide
ISBN 978-1-86144-049-5 £8.99

Applying to University The Essential Guide
ISBN 978-1-86144-052-5 £8.99

ADHD The Essential Guide
ISBN 978-1-86144-060-0 £8.99

Student Cookbook - Healthy Eating The Essential Guide
ISBN 978-1-86144-061-7 £8.99

Stress The Essential Guide
ISBN 978-1-86144-054-9 £8.99

Adoption and Fostering A Parent's Guide
ISBN 978-1-86144-056-3 £8.99

Special Educational Needs A Parent's Guide
ISBN 978-1-86144-057-0 £8.99

The Pill An Essential Guide
ISBN 978-1-86144-058-7 £8.99

University A Survival Guide
ISBN 978-1-86144-072-3 £8.99

Diabetes The Essential Guide
ISBN 978-1-86144-059-4 £8.99

View the full range at **www.need2knowbooks.co.uk**. To order our title
call **01733 898103**, email **sales@n2kbooks.com** or visit the website

Need - 2 - Know, Remus House, Coltsfoot Drive, Peterborough, PE2 9JX